THE
INDUSTRIAL ATHLETE
OPERATING SYSTEM

WHERE HUMAN PERFORMANCE EMPOWERS INDUSTRY 4.0

by

Mark Lamoncha
Tim Figley

Forword by Jim Tressel

THE INDUSTRIAL ATHLETE OPERATING SYSTEM:
WHERE HUMAN PERFORMANCE EMPOWERS INDUSTRY 4.0

Copyright © 2023 by Mark Lamoncha and Tim Figley

All rights reserved. No part of this book may be reproduced or transmitted in any form or by any means without written permission from the author.

ISBN: 979-8-9889339-0-8

Printed in the United States of America

TABLE OF CONTENTS

COMMITMENT TO UNLEASHING MY POTENTIAL 7

THE INDUSTRIAL ATHLETE: MORE THAN A METAPHOR 9

    CHAPTER 1: THE MINDSET THAT DRIVES PERFORMANCE 15
    CHAPTER 2: CHANGES IN THE WORK WORLD 23
    CHAPTER 3: TEAMWORK AS A COMPETITIVE ADVANTAGE 27
    CHAPTER 4: THE INDUSTRIAL ATHLETE OPERATING SYSTEM FRAMEWORK 33

PART 1: FROM WORKPLACE TO PERFORMANCE CENTER 39

    CHAPTER 5: FROM CHAOS TO CLARITY 43
    CHAPTER 6: FROM APATHY TO ENGAGEMENT 49
    CHAPTER 7: FROM FOURTH-QUARTER FAILURE TO A WINNING SCOREBOARD 55

PART 2: FROM A TUG-OF-WAR TO A WIN-WIN CULTURE 61

    CHAPTER 8: FROM US VS. THEM TO WIN-WIN 65
    CHAPTER 9: FROM SUBTLE SABOTAGE TO TRUSTED TEAMWORK 71
    CHAPTER 10: FROM DOWNWARD SPIRAL TO UPWARD SYNERGY 77

PART 3: FROM EMPLOYEE TO INDUSTRIAL ATHLETE 89

    CHAPTER 11: FROM SURVIVING TO THRIVING 95
    CHAPTER 12: FROM DISENGAGED WORKER TO TALENTED TEAM MEMBER 103
    CHAPTER 13: FROM UNMET EXPECTATIONS TO PEAK PERFORMANCE 111

PART 4: FROM BOSS TO COACH 121

    CHAPTER 14: FROM COMMAND AND CONTROL TO INSPIRE AND TRUST 127
    CHAPTER 15: FROM TASKMASTER TO SERVANT LEADER 135
    CHAPTER 16: FROM MICROMANAGER TO MULTIPLIER 143

AFTERWORD: HOW TO TRANSFORM 155

    APPENDIX A: ASSESSMENT 157
    APPENDIX B: THE HUMTOWN STORY 163
    ABOUT MARK LAMONCHA 167
    ABOUT DR. TIM FIGLEY 168

TABLE OF FIGURES

Figure 1: The Four Transformations 11
Figure 2: Pay-Rate Jail™ vs. Visual Earnings™ 20
Figure 3: Four Changes and Four Challenges in Our World . 25
Figure 4: Mindset, Behavior, Results 29
Figure 5: Industrial Age vs. Industrial Athlete 31
Figure 6: The Four Transformations Expanded 33
Figure 7: Workplace Transformation 39
Figure 8: Comparing Workplace to Performance Center 42
Figure 9: From Chaos to Clarity 43
Figure 10: Visual Earnings ™ System Gamification 51
Figure 11: Visual Earnings™ Change 57
Figure 12: GAME Plan 59
Figure 13: Cultural Transformation Defined 61
Figure 14: Tug-of-War vs. Win-Win Culture 64
Figure 15: Culture Spectrum 67
Figure 16: VES Percentage Chart 69
Figure 17: Tug-of-War Culture 72
Figure 18: Upward Synergy vs. Downward Spiral 77
Figure 19: Inside Out ValYou Process 79
Figure 20: The Multiplier Effect 83
Figure 21: Win-Win Continuum 87
Figure 22: Employee Transformation Defined 89
Figure 23: Mindset, Engagement, Performance 92
Figure 24: Employee and Industrial Athlete Comparison 93
Figure 25: THRIVE 360 100
Figure 26: Interest, Purpose, Passion, Engagement.............. 105
Figure 27: Talent Match 106
Figure 28: Before Talent Example 48% 108

Figure 29: After Talent Example 86% 109
Figure 30: Top 10 List 113
Figure 31: Yerkes-Dodson Performance Curve 114
Figure 32: Trust/Performance Matrix 119
Figure 33: Management Transformation Defined 121
Figure 34: The Scrap and the Eagle...................................... 123
Figure 35: Boss vs Coach Approach...................................... 124
Figure 36: Servant Leadership Framework 138
Figure 37: Humtown Team Members' Thank You 140
Figure 38: Monthly Sales Team Member Multiplication 151
Figure 39: Coach Continuum... 153

COMMITMENT TO UNLEASHING MY POTENTIAL

Dear Valued Reader,

It is an honor to have this opportunity to connect with you. As I sit here, pen in hand, I am humbled by the magnitude of the life experiences that have shaped you into who you are today. Even though I may not have the privilege of knowing every detail or fully grasping the depth of your journey, I want you to know that I am committed to embarking on this meaningful endeavor with you.

I hope this book will serve as an instrument of illumination for you. I want the words to resonate deeply and inspire you to uncover the extraordinary layers that define you and the people around you. Each revelation and insight within these chapters aims to uncover the hidden brilliance within you and your team, propelling you toward the greatest version of yourself with every new endeavor.

Importantly, this book is more than a collection of our stories; it invites you to write down your thoughts, sketch your reflections, and create your own action plan for you and your organization. Think of this as a space to outline your personal and organizational growth plan.

As we embark on this remarkable journey, let us join our pens as co-authors of your future story. Together, we will navigate a path of discovery and growth. I am privileged to intertwine my thoughts with yours, nurturing the potential for transformative change with each chapter.

Your commitment below confirms as you read through these perspectives presented in our story and the words and stories intersect in real time with your life, that they would allow you to become the best version of yourself in a team or as you serve a team as a coach.

_____

Your Signature, for becoming your best self

Mark Lamoncha

Mark Lamoncha, my support to your best success

FOREWORD

Mark Lamoncha and Tim Figley have developed a winning "Game Plan" for business and industry that can create success for ALL groups and teams. Believing that a group is insignificant until EVERY individual is greatly valued by the TEAM, Mark and Tim have a proven formula for your TEAM's success.

The journey in this book begins with transforming the "workplace" into a "performance center" that can raise the excitement and productivity level of everyone. Developing a "Win-Win Culture" instills camaraderie for everyone to come together each day. Our championship TEAMS at Ohio State and Youngstown State could not wait to be together each day to see just how good we could become. We learned that when we came together with a common cause, we could experience greatness.

Finally, developing a connection between the coaches and Industrial Athletes results in the care that will allow the entire organization to reach its full potential.

Dig in, study their system, apply the principles, and your TEAM can become a championship TEAM. As we all know, great things do not happen overnight. The hallmark of excellence, the test of greatness, is consistency. It is time to perform, time to coach, time to love, time to genuinely care, and time to WIN!!

Jim Tressel

Head Football Coach, Youngstown State University and
The Ohio State University, Five-Time National Champion
Past President, Youngstown State University.

THE INDUSTRIAL ATHLETE: MORE THAN A METAPHOR

What if our team members could be as engaged in the workplace as our favorite athletes are on the playing field? To see people truly engaged, watch them put their whole selves into outperforming the competition to win a coveted trophy. Watch the fans, their faces painted, wearing their favorite team's jersey at their favorite college football game. They are cheering with their friends, having the time of their lives.

But what happens when we follow them to work the next week? Are they as excited? Engaged? Committed?

Imagine creating a high-performing organization where everyone engages with their whole being while working for the love of it. That is exactly what we set out to do.

We asked,

"Is there a way to create a workplace that facilitates engaged team members to create better organizational performance?"

Yes, there is! Transforming your workplace into a performance center can motivate people to unleash their talents, interests, passion, and teamwork. As a natural consequence, sales revenue, net profit margin, and customer retention tend to increase.

This book reveals how you can take the same concepts that a successful athletic environment creates for players and use them to create better engagement and higher productivity among your workforce for greater organizational performance.

THE INDUSTRIAL ATHLETE OPERATING SYSTEM

The **Industrial Athlete Operating System** focuses on four areas of transformation for your organization: workplace performance, culture, management, and employees. This comprehensive and extremely effective talent management system has transformed a small company teetering on the edge of bankruptcy into a fiercely competitive, rapidly growing, and dominant player in the metal casting industry.

The **Industrial Athlete Operating System** recognizes that human potential is the most valuable business asset–because *nobody has ever created anything better than a human being.*

It has been said that we have emerged into the Fourth Industrial Revolution, referred to as Industry 4.0.[1] There is a great need to shift from the first Industrial Age mentality of managing people like things, to an updated "People 4.0" that revolutionizes how we lead people into greater engagement and performance.[2]

As technology and AI reshapes the world, pundits fear that the value of human potential will be diminished in the workplace. In response, the Industrial Athlete Operating System shows how the most profitable and forward-thinking organizations can enable human potential to create organizational success.

This system taps into the science of human performance to get everyone rowing in the same direction so that the whole organization can function with synergy.

Envision a Swiss watch. Since the whole is greater than the sum of the parts, every gear is important.[3] If one gear malfunctions, the entire watch stops. Similarly, this system recognizes that the people who are the lifeblood of your company have unique value and untapped energy in their ability to create value together.

The Industrial Athlete Operating System implements four mindset shifts that transform workplaces from the ordinary to the extraordinary by transforming employees into high-performing Industrial Athletes, as illustrated in Figure 1. By optimizing their experiences, organizations go from surviving to thriving. Each essential transformation will be explored in detail for practical application to any organization.

1. **The Workplace Transformation**:
   From *Workplace* to *Performance Center*
2. **The Culture Transformation:**
   From *Tug-of-War Culture* to a *Win-Win Culture*
3. **The Employee Transformation:**
   From *Employee* to *Industrial Athlete*
4. **The Managerial Transformation**:
   From *Boss* to *Coach*

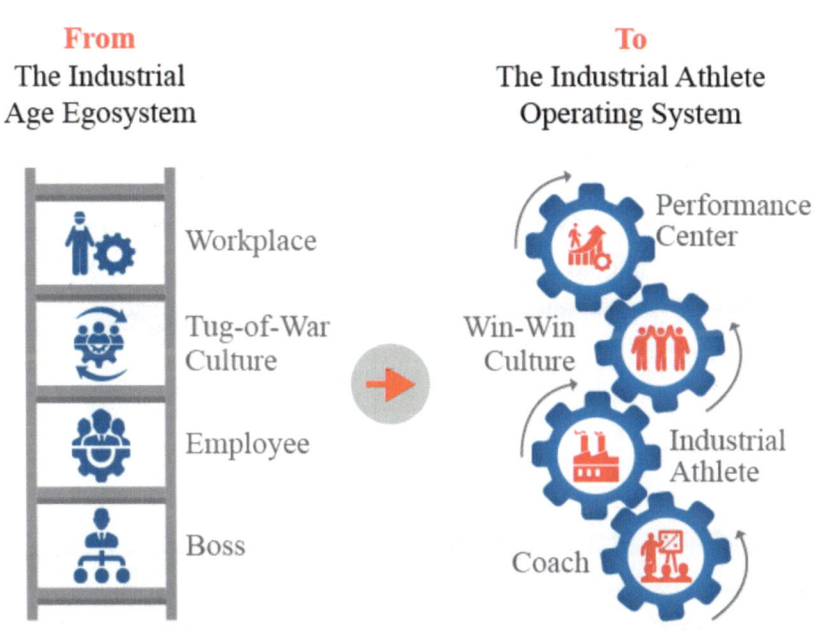

Figure 1: The Four Transformations

At the beginning of each part of the book you will find a progressive variation of Figure 1. These figures are there to serve as a visual cue as we make our way through the four transformations.

THE HUMTOWN EXPERIENCE

Humtown Products™, a family-owned company based in Columbiana, Ohio, manufactures 3D printed and conventional cores and molds for the foundry industry. The company makes parts for the agriculture, mining, manufacturing, transportation, defense, and public utility industries. Humtown could be described like any successful midsize American manufacturer, at face value. Yet, the company now has an international impact.

Mark Lamoncha and his team transformed the business that was on the verge of bankruptcy in 2008 to winning the **2020 Manufacturer of the Year Award** from the **National Association of Manufacturers** in the Small/Medium Enterprise, Engineering and Production Technology and Talent Management categories. He had created a patented **Visual Earnings™ System** (VES) that dramatically improves productivity by enhancing the human skills and potential of Humtown's workforce through technological innovation, data science, and gamification.

Mark explains,

"Our Visual Earnings™ System helped us create a win-win culture that empowered everybody to have a voice and determine their financial destiny."

He recognized that increasing innovation to enhance the company's performance would benefit both the business and team members on the shop floor. Designing a system that had gaming components aligned with accountability measures that linked to financial rewards, caused an increase in performance and engagement.

The innovation did not stop there. Mark, along with organizational consultant Dr. Tim Figley, have taken these patented ideas to the next level to create the Industrial Athlete Operating System. This method enhances the value of people in the workplace while simultaneously elevating organizational performance.

Mark says,

"At Humtown, we once had over 70 percent employee turnover. We knew the relational pain and the financial costs of disengaged people. We wanted to turn our company around and give our team members a shared language and vision of success."

This vision of success has become the Industrial Athlete Operating System and is revealed in this book. As we analyzed the transformation at Humtown Products™ and compared it to a winning sports team, we realized that the relationship between sports performance and business performance is more than just a metaphor. It is a language and a way of life that creates greater energy to fulfill the needs of people in our communities.

Youngstown State University's football team proved that the impact could go beyond the 100-yard football field to inspire and lift an entire community. We personally gleaned wisdom from the coaching prowess of Jim Tressel, the five-time national championship coach and University President. Since junior high, Tim has learned from Tressel–from his pre-game locker room football speeches to his coaching and leadership classes based on the principles from his best-selling book, *The Winners Manual*.

Humtown partnered with Youngstown State when Tressel became president. In Humtown's Locker Room meetings, Tressel has shared the same winning principles that earned Ohio State their first championship in nearly 40 years. As a result, our collaborative focus combines Humtown's award-winning systems and demonstrates how you, too, can transform your organization.

CHAPTER 1:
THE MINDSET THAT DRIVES PERFORMANCE

If you travel to the Lighthouse Point Bar and Grille on Lake Sumter in The Villages, Florida, not only will you find the New England clam chowder and Maine lobster roll, but you will also find a sign above the bar that says,

"NE 3 ATL 28 with 2:12 in the 3rd Quarter."

This sign is a visual reminder of the Super Bowl when the New England Patriots were losing to the Atlanta Falcons by almost four touchdowns going into the fourth quarter.

After three dismal quarters and their backs against the wall, many fans had left the game or turned their televisions off, thinking it was over. They would not have been wrong in most cases, since no team had ever recovered from more than a ten-point deficit to win the Super Bowl.

However, Super Bowl 51 would be unlike any other. Fans began to text each other in disbelief, and those who had turned their TVs off turned them back on as the game became competitive again. They could not take their eyes off what was once thought a boring blowout. The suspense took more than 100 million television viewers into overtime. Quarterback Tom Brady would lead his team from 25 points down to the greatest comeback in Super Bowl history for a game-winning victory, 34 to 28.

What prompted this engaging, high-achieving performance? We believe four transformations occurred between the first three quarters and the final quarter.

1. A scoreboard and a time clock were winding down, creating pressure to perform. The sense of urgency motivates.
2. The team worked together more cohesively than during the first three quarters. The presence of teamwork motivates.

3. The coaching staff called the right plays. The quality of trusted leadership motivates.
4. The individual athletes mounted a monumental comeback. The focus to win motivates.

These are the same four transformations that created a U-shaped turnaround at Humtown™ from the 2008 losses to the **2020 NAM Small Business Manufacturer of the Year**.

Think about it. Many of us have been inspired by watching athletes swim, run, row, jump, or cycle in a highly competitive race. They put themselves all in to reach the gold. And it is not just the professionals and Olympians. Athletics tend to bond people together to create a community. We see athletes of all ages who love to train, practice, get coached, work together on a team, and put themselves out there for the love of the game.

Not only do the participants benefit, but the fans also love it. They pay big dollars and fill stadiums to witness a competitive-spirited, edge-of-your-seat game and cheer for a winning result. Nothing sells more tickets and attracts more customers than a high-stakes, high-performing athletic event. The Olympics, for example, have worldwide appeal. It is one of the few remaining places where young people witness the great qualities of the human spirit, from challenging work and dedication to patriotism to teamwork, passion, and determination. We watch the Olympics not because we are enthralled with bobsled or ski jumping, but because we see these young people from around the world in a crucible of stress, rising above it all.

Another example is the Super Bowl. Twenty-nine of the thirty most-watched television broadcasts are NFL Super Bowls.[4]

They have consistently generated more than 100 million viewers per game since 2010. The National Football League created these stratospheric numbers by focusing on four performance-based assumptions to drive success:

> **Performance**: Their "workplace" is actually a PERFORMANCE FIELD with clear rules, boundaries, and scoreboards clarifying what is needed to win the game.
>
> **Win-Win Culture**: They have created a culture with a team-based reward system and pay-for-performance incentives. Teams work together to achieve their highest goals and receive a trophy that their entire city can celebrate.
>
> **Coaches**: Instead of managers who watch over people, they are COACHES who get the most out of the players and create winning results.
>
> **Athletes**: Instead of employees who come to work and get paid for their time, they are ATHLETES who engage, practice, and get paid for high-performing outcomes.

What kind of performance results would you create if you engaged team members as if they were athletes instead of managing them like mere workers? How do you suppose it would impact your organizational performance?

These are the questions we asked at Humtown when we went from 226 employees to 17 and were on the brink of bankruptcy in 2008. We desperately needed a comeback win.

Mark tells of a time when he and his wife Sheri were watching their boys play hockey.

He says,

> *"I would take my notebook and work on business until the game started. While they played, I noticed the engagement level, coaching style, and team performance. It dawned on me, 'What if we engaged in our work as much as the kids out on the ice?'"*

The recession of 2008 brought disaster to Humtown, as it did to many other manufacturing businesses. The entire metal casting industry saw a 70 percent drop in sales, causing many companies to go out of business. Our sales dropped precipitously. Our net profit margin was a negative 13 percent. Our local Small Business Development Center, seeing that we were headed in the wrong direction, calculated what they anticipated as an even bigger loss. The shrinking profit margins made us realize that we could go out of business.

It was the end of the third quarter, and with our backs against the wall like the Patriots in Super Bowl 51, we needed a game plan to get us back on our feet–or game over. Rather than give up, we saw this as an opportunity to implement a combination of technology and talent management initiatives to empower our team members and save the business from bankruptcy. We realized from our own experience that employees often seek their real engagement and fulfillment on the weekends. Yet, at work, they had the unenthusiastic attitude of "same stuff, different day."

As we examined why that was and wondered if we could create a new engaging work environment where people *want* to go, we had to look at ourselves in the mirror and discover what kind of mindset had led us to this point.

MINDSETS AT HUMTOWN BEFORE TRANSFORMATION

1. **Workplace Mindset**
   Our performance mindset was lacking. Previously 152 employees were needed to generate $247,000 a week in manufacturing sales. Yielded sales were $60,894 per team member.

2. **Culture Mindset**
   We had a tug-of-war mindset. Our staff worked 8-hour days, for 6 days a week. Every moment was focused on production from a survival mindset, and everyone was continually drained. As for our culture, we did not believe that we had the time to prioritize that element. Team members were tired from working longer hours, and they felt stuck. The workforce felt they *had* to be there rather than *wanting* to be there.

3. **Management Mindset**
   The norm for our leadership was putting out fires and micromanaging people. Our leadership style back then was akin to one from the early Industrial Age, a command-and-control mindset: "Show up, and we will tell you what to do." Unfortunately, people were disempowered. We were constricting their potential without knowing it.

4. **Employee Mindset**
   We realized that we unintentionally viewed our employees as objects, only there to generate company profits. We did not value their personhood from a 360-degree view. Therefore, employee turnover was 70 percent–which proved to be an ongoing problem, creating 50 percent of our labor costs.

When analyzing what brought out the best in people to perform at the highest levels, we looked to competitive sports. That is where we saw maximum engagement and highest performance. Also, we noticed employees excited over the entertainment value of fantasy football, March Madness, and watching others play in the game.

As a result, we developed the Visual Earnings™ System so that our team members could *play in the game* through real-time performance scoreboards rather than just watching the game! We changed how we viewed our team members and the language we used by coaching them instead of supervising them. This approach was opposed to what we had known before because our production staff used to be locked in an hourly rate, limited in their potential in what Mark termed "Pay-Rate Jail™."

Mark describes Pay-Rate Jail™:

"If your rate is pre-determined, you do not hold the key to increasing it. The boss holds the key to whether you will make more money or not, hence the jail analogy."

Figure 2 illustrates how the **Visual Earnings™ System** is diametrically opposed to Pay-Rate Jail™.

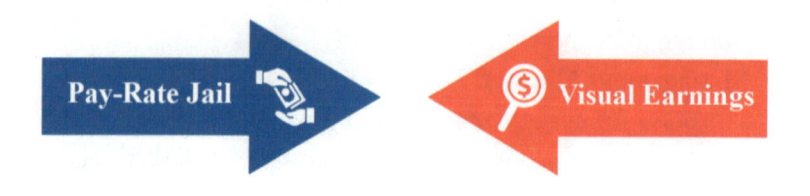

Figure 2: Pay-Rate Jail™ vs. Visual Earnings™

The real-time feedback provided by the Visual Earnings™ System caused their performance to increase, and so did the company's profits. However, creating the VES was only part of the solution. Our Industrial Athletes had to be surrounded by a complete human operating system to transform our company.

So, we made four transformations in our approach that began to bring about the changes needed.

HUMTOWN'S FOUR TRANSFORMATIONS

1. **The Workplace Transformation**:
   From Workplace to Performance Center
   We shifted from a workplace filled with unclear assumptions to a performance center with a winning strategy, playbook, performance game plan, and visual scorekeeping to facilitate high performance.

2. **The Culture Transformation:**
   From Tug-of-War Culture to Win-Win Culture
   Only *realized* culture impacts a team's performance level. We shifted from a tug-of-war culture to a win-win high-trust culture.

3. **The Employee Transformation:**
   From Employee to Industrial Athlete
   To engage employees to perform optimally, we shifted away from valuing them for production alone, which led to disengagement, underperformance, and burnout. Rather, we empowered them to think, engage, practice, and perform together like top athletes.

4. **The Managerial Transformation**:
   From Boss to Coach
   To support team members to perform together like Industrial Athletes, we shifted from a boss mindset that led to mistrust and disempowerment to a coaching mindset that serves, listens, inspires, builds teams, and facilitates high trust.

PERFORMANCE RESULTS

"The downside is that a person spends $20 to watch that hero instead of being that hero himself."

–Patrick Bet David

We released our team members from finding their fulfillment in watching athletes on the weekends to becoming the athletes themselves. We gave each Industrial Athlete the keys to get out of Pay-Rate Jail™ and determine how productive they wanted to be. They learned how to keep score and become the chief determiners of their financial destiny. These strides increased our profitability significantly in the first 24 months. Our results were as follows:

1. **Performance Center Results**
   The impact of shifting from the Workplace to a Performance Center increased our net profit margins by nearly 40 percent.

2. **Culture Results**
   Our collective productivity skyrocketed from an average $60,000 to up to $400,000 in monthly production sales per team member because of shifting from a tug-of-war culture to a win-win culture. More importantly, that created a new degree of engagement at every level.

3. **Industrial Athlete Results**
   After shifting from employees to Industrial Athletes, our team members increased their performance results and paychecks from between 150 to 400 percent.

4. **Coaching Results**
   Our staff turnover dropped from 70 percent to under 10 percent once we shifted from a boss mindset to a coaching mindset.

CHAPTER 2:
CHANGES IN THE WORK WORLD

Now is the time for a new way of thinking about our workplace. The world of work and industry is shifting radically.[5] We are now in a connected world where the shift is happening faster, continuously, and unpredictably.

Swift and continuous technological advances create a business environment where video meetings, smart technology, and social media are universal. Events such as the 2008 recession, pandemics, and global conflicts have increased the sense of turbulence, risk, and unpredictability.

New terms are created to describe this. For example, international shifts can be described using the acronym VUCA, which stands for Volatile, Uncertain, Complex, and Ambiguous. This state of fluctuation has replaced the sense of confidence and stability.

TRANSFORMATIVE SHIFTS OF A WORLD IN TRANSITION

As the workforce undergoes a sea change, the need to engage team members and create high-performing organizations has never been more important or relevant. Yet, as the world changes, the workplace often still manages people like we were in the earlier Industrial Age. Organizations are underperforming because they are not harnessing their team members' full performance capabilities.

Our people are our greatest resource, but they may not have been allowed to unleash the potential, talent, creativity, and ingenuity they are capable of, leaving our greatest competitive advantage locked up and our profit centers stifled.

New team members come into the work environment well-intended but sometimes traumatized by earlier life events and previous work experiences. As a result, organizations generally do not know how to lead this incoming workforce; instead, they remain stuck in an outdated leadership style. This way of leading people disengages individual and organizational performance and negatively impacts productivity, quality, and safety.

The incoming generation calls for better work-life balance and fair compensation upon joining the workforce. They also want clear goals, an overhaul of reward and recognition systems, and greater work fulfillment. These changes will require a new management operating system.

These are not the only influences of change moving through our world, impacting our workplaces and individual lives. As shown in Figure 3, we have identified four major changes in our work world today, causing four organizational challenges. If our people are not fully engaged, how much are organizations losing on their talent, intelligence, innovation, and results? How do we encourage the necessary innovation, engagement, teamwork, and performance from our people?

The Four Changes	The Four Challenges
The Workplace Changes: The emergence of the 4th Industrial Revolution, digitization and workplace capabilities and consumer expectations.	**The Workplace Challenge:** According to a Harris Poll, only 12 percent of people know how their tasks align with organizational goals.
The Culture Changes: People's compositions and views have become more diverse. Diverse and hybrid work styles, worldviews, ethnicities, and backgrounds impact the organizational culture and team cohesiveness.	**The Culture Challenge:** 80 percent of people believe their culture needs to change.
The Employee Changes: Technological changes have made the world smaller, allowing people to work from anywhere. This has created a global war for talent and tipped the balance of power toward the worker.	**The Employee Challenge:** The Gallup polling company revealed in their state of the workplace poll that 85 percent of employees are disengaged, costing US companies nearly $1 trillion annually.
The Management Changes: With an anticipated workforce of 55 percent Millennials and Generation Zs by 2025, we can expect a change in workplace norms, behavior, and expectations.	**The Management Challenge:** According to Gallup, 70 percent of the variance of disengagement is from the manager, yet CareerBuilder.com reveals that 58 percent of managers do not receive training.

Figure 3: Four Changes and Four Challenges in Our World

CHAPTER 3:
TEAMWORK AS A COMPETITIVE ADVANTAGE

We started with the changes. Then, we explored the underlying challenges that involve deeply embedded mindsets in the workplace. Now, we need context for a solution.

The Fourth Industrial Revolution emphasizes smart automation and interconnectivity. Our workplaces today have intelligent machines, the Internet, artificial intelligence, and robotics. Also known as Industry 4.0, this time of change hyper-focuses on transformative technology as it is often thought to provide us with our greatest advantage.

However, think about an organization's greatest competitive advantage when considering a thriving business or industry. How did it achieve its success? Was it innovative technology? The perfect business system?

In most cases, these factors could have contributed to the business or industry's favorable outcome. Still, the **most crucial factor** is the *people* who created the success. No matter what technology exists, human potential will always be the greatest energy and source of creation on earth. Without the person who created the innovation and the people who operated the organization to make the concept a reality, it would all be irrelevant.

As groundbreaking as the introduction of the iPhone was in 2007, it would not have happened without the turned-on, tapped-in, innovative ingenuity of Steve Jobs and Apple's collaborative team. As Patrick Lencioni said,

> *"Not finance. Not strategy. Not technology. Teamwork remains the ultimate competitive advantage because it is so powerful and rare."*[6]

Therefore, we will find our greatest competitive advantage by understanding how people work together in a human operating system to increase organizational performance.

IDENTIFYING A HUMAN OPERATING SYSTEM

According to W. Edwards Deming, the guru of Total Quality Management (TQM), a system is:

"a network of interdependent components that work together to accomplish a common aim." [7]

We are acquainted with such business systems as enterprise management, lead generation, marketing, and fiscal management systems, and we know how to make them run effectively. Unfortunately, we are often not as effective in optimizing our human operating system. Similar to a business system, the human operating system is the interconnection of how people relate and work together to accomplish an organization's shared aim.

The human operating system is the communication pipeline that accomplishes the desired objectives. Think of it like a computer network. We all know what happens when our computer network goes down: we can't process payments, access our email, find customer orders, etc. For the human operating system to perform optimally, we need to have an open communication channel to harness the people's collective talent so they can help increase the performance and bottom line of the organization. The outcome for individuals is elevated instead of diminished.

COMPONENTS OF THE HUMAN OPERATING SYSTEM: MINDSET, BEHAVIOR, PERFORMANCE RESULTS

The human operating system starts with a mindset, a pattern of thinking of both the individual players and the collective members of an organization. A McKinsey study finds that failure to recognize and shift mindsets can stall the change efforts of the entire organization.[8] A pattern

CHAPTER 3: TEAMWORK AS A COMPETITIVE ADVANTAGE

of thinking is based on underlying beliefs or assumptions, and beliefs contribute to behaviors.

The relationship between Performance, Behavior, and Mindset is illustrated in Figure 4.

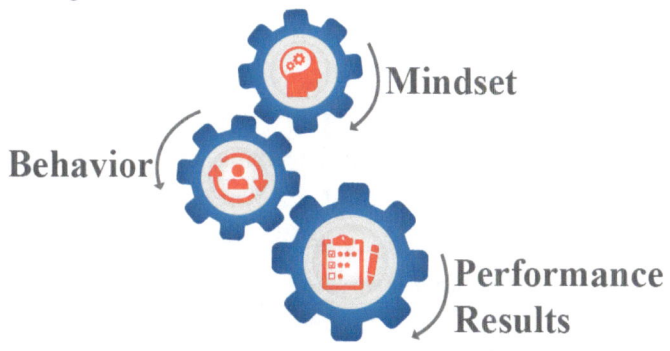

Figure 4: Mindset, Behavior, Results

Behavior patterns are like habits. These habits impact the culture, the speed at which things are done, and the organization's performance. Behavior patterns are what contribute to organizational results.

Clearly, the habits of individuals on the job affect the outcome for a business. Performance results are the measures of the success or failure of a business. They demonstrate the quality and value of products and services that lead to employee engagement and stakeholder satisfaction. In other words, mindset contributes to behavior, and behavior contributes to performance.

TYPES OF HUMAN OPERATING SYSTEMS

Each organization has a human operating system that prioritizes either the value of people above profits or the value of profits above people. The system that values people above profits tends to create higher profits in the long run.

Firms of Endearment researchers studied companies that honored and created value for all *stakeholders* rather than just *stock shareholders*. The performance of these Firms of Endearment over a 15-year span had a 14-

to-1 higher cumulative return than the average company on the S&P 500. These companies earned larger profits for all their stakeholders.

If that research verifies the value of people, then goodwill is the primary currency of a human operating system. The profits produced are like looking in the rearview mirror because they are the lagging results. Think about that natural consequence. When people are valued, the overflow is financial profit, not the other way around. Valuing machines and profits above people leads to surviving and not thriving because it locks up human potential and goodwill. Not unlike killing the goose that lays the golden eggs, it will not be as effective in the long run.

In his book *The Ultimate Question,* Fred Reichheld says,

"Whenever the customer feels misled, mistreated, ignored, or coerced, profits from customers are bad. Bad profits are about extracting value from customers, not creating value." [9]

In a human operating system, when we extract value from team members for profits alone rather than creating value *with* them, it creates bad profits. When organizations function within an "operating system" of scarcity, indulgence, and ego, then that characterizes the out-of-date Industrial Age Egosystem. Furthermore, the mindset of the Industrial Age Egosystem views people like machines, as objects to be used; this results in disengagement and creates bad profits.

The mindset of the Industrial Athlete Operating System is to nurture the inherent value within people, which creates full engagement. Good profits are the result. Changing from a boss and employee workplace with a tug-of-war culture to a coach and Industrial Athlete performance center with a win-win culture creates "good profits" that benefit all.

Reichheld further explains,

"Good profits benefit both the customer and the business. This occurs when a business creates value for the customer, and they keep coming back for more. These customers tell their friends and family to also do business with you. They become your promoters

and create good profit for the company and create growth that is sustainable."

A human operating system that values people first creates a thriving, profitable organization because people operate and benefit from the system. Within a healthy, functional human operating system, each person has intrinsic value, worth, and purpose.

Now, at Humtown we see all people for their real value–not just what they can do, but who they are. We started with our Humtown team members in our endeavor to meet all our stakeholders' functional, emotional, and social needs. We coined the term *ValYou*, reinforcing that our greatest value is not our physical property or machine assets; rather, our greatest asset is the ValYou in our people.

It was a shift from the value *of* people to the ValYou *in* people. From that moment on, we trusted that if we took care of our team members, they would care for us.

The value of people is in them all the time, not just when they are at work. We no longer hire just for our purposes, but for our team members' purposes.

Mark has often been known to say that we have television shows like "This Old House" or "This Old Car" that talk about restoring a house or car, but we need to restore our greatest value and that is our people.

	The Industrial Age Egosystem	The Industrial Athlete Operating System
Mindset	Treat people like machines	Value people above profits and machines
Behavior	Disengagement	Full Engagement
Performance Results	Bad Profits	Good Profits

Figure 5: Industrial Age vs. Industrial Athlete

To execute an effective strategy, a business owner must be able to impart the idea without too much resistance through the coaches and people performing on the job. At the same time, people within the organization are usually the closest to the action and have multiple ideas for improvement. We may find that they have a great idea. If there is an open channel of communication, we regularly receive innovative ideas to help us all win.

THE NEED FOR A HUMAN OPERATING SYSTEM FRAMEWORK

A visual framework that reveals an accurate human operating system will help us identify the organizational outcomes we are receiving. Stephen Covey stated,

"The power of an accurate paradigm lies in its ability to explain and predict."

The Industrial Athlete Operating System is a clear framework that can help us assess and overcome our greatest challenges. We use this framework to create a human operating system that will, in turn, create a dynamic, high-performing organization.

CHAPTER 4:
THE INDUSTRIAL ATHLETE OPERATING SYSTEM FRAMEWORK

From
The Industrial Age Egosystem

To
The Industrial Athlete Operating System

Workplace
- ○ Fourth Quarter
- △ Apathy
- □ Chaos

Structural Transformation →

Performance Center
- ○ Winning
- △ Scoreboard Engagement
- □ Clarity

Tug-of-War Culture
- ○ Downward Spiral
- △ Subtle Sabotage
- □ Us vs. Them

Social Transformation →

Win-Win Culture
- ○ Upward Spiral
- △ Trusted Teamwork
- □ Win-Win

Employee
- ○ Unmet Expectations
- △ Disengaged Worker
- □ Surviving

Personal Transformation →

Industrial Athlete
- ○ Peak Performance
- △ Talented Performance
- □ Thriving

Boss
- ○ Micro-Managed
- △ Task Master
- □ Command and Control

Management Transformation →

Coach
- ○ Multiplier Servant
- △ Leader Inspire and
- □ Trust

LEGEND
- ○ Performance
- △ Results
- □ Behaviour

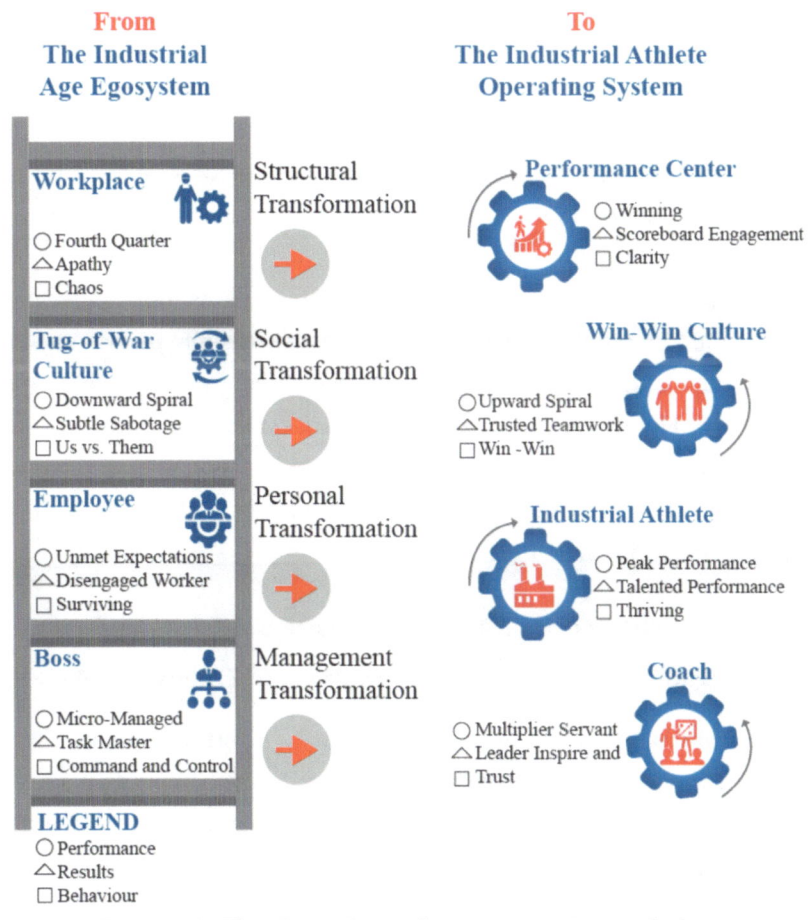

Figure 6: The Four Transformations Expanded

Four transformations are needed. Our framework deals specifically with these changes with workplace, culture, employee, and managerial transitions, going from… to….

The word *transformation* means:

"*a thorough or dramatic change in form or appearance.*[10]

We will not see different results without changing the design of our organizations to reflect dramatic transformation. As Arthur Jones says,

"*All organizations are perfectly designed to get the results they get.*"

The key to creating success will be shifting from the Industrial Age Egosystem to the Industrial Athlete Operating System.

Climbing up the corporate ladder is still the prevalent paradigm for success. From rigid, hierarchical organization models, status, individual incentives, information flow, power, and influence reflect their core values.

However, the workplace today is undergoing change, shifting away from the traditional, hierarchical, one-size-fits-all paradigm of the corporate ladder and toward a more collaborative, interconnected approach. Humtown Coach Brian Cyphert compared an organization to the gears on his watch that need to work together. When the gears interact, then workplace, culture, employee, and managerial transformation occur, as depicted in Figure 6.

THE FOUR TRANSFORMATIONS WITHIN THE
INDUSTRIAL ATHLETE OPERATING SYSTEM FRAMEWORK

Setting the stage for the mindset that drives performance in Chapter 1 led to changes in the work world in Chapter 2. The competitive advantage of a positive human operating system in Chapters 3 and 4 initiated Humtown's Industrial Athlete Operating System. In the remaining Chapters, 5 through 16, the specific details of each transition of the transformation can be categorized into four parts, which make up the four Parts of this book.

Referring to Figure 6 and the consecutive figures at the beginning of each part may help to clarify our position on the road to complete transformation.

Part 1. The Workplace-to-Performance CenterTransformation

Part 1 in the journey is understanding the transformation from Workplace to Performance Center. This is the Workplace Transformation. In sports, the roles on the playing field are clearly defined. There is accountability if someone steps out of line, and the scoreboard urges the players and excites the fans. The team with the most points wins; it is as simple as that. This transformation is accomplished by moving from chaos to clarity, from apathy to engagement, and from fourth-quarter failure to a winning scoreboard.

Chapter 5 begins the transformation by shifting the mindset from chaos to clarity. Without clarity, people cannot function to the fullest, resulting in a faulty foundation within the organization. We reveal tips and ideas to bring clarity to organizational purpose through an MVP playbook and a GAME Plan.

Chapter 6 shifts from apathy to engagement. The organization needs performance scoreboards to create engagement after the MVP playbook and GAME Plan have clarified things.

Chapter 7 shifts an organization from fourth-quarter failure to winning scoreboards. Developing clarity and creating engagement through performance scoreboards will create winning results.

Part 2. The Tug-of-War-to-Team Transformation

In Part 2, we are shifting from a tug-of-war culture to a win-win culture. This transitions the organization for a Culture Transformation.

Chapter 8 shifts the underlying pervading mindset of us versus them to a win-win mindset and shows viable benefits.

Chapter 9 then reveals how subtle sabotage results from an us vs. them mentality and explains how to create the more advantageous behavior of trusted teamwork.

Trusted teamwork will lead an organization into upward synergy, as revealed in Chapter 10.

Part 3. The Employee-to-Industrial-Athlete Transformation

In Part 3, the Personal Transformation challenges employees to view themselves as Industrial Athletes. Once we discover our unique selves, we can have an unclouded vision of what to do.

Chapter 11 defines what survival mode is like. The shift to treating employees as human beings and caring about them from a 360-degree perspective allows everyone to thrive.

Chapter 12 reveals that giving someone a task just because they are able and available does not make it the right fit. Focusing on production alone and not personal skillsets will often result in disengaged workers. Talented performers are those whose interests, thinking styles, and behavioral traits match their job position.

Chapter 13 reveals that if employees work in a job that does not match their innate talents and skills, they will always have unmet expectations. When employees are allowed to grow and function within their natural skillset, they are in the peak performance zone.

Part 4. The Boss-to-Coach Transformation

In Part 4, we examine the transformation from boss to coach for a Management Transformation.

In Chapter 14, the old command-and-control leadership style is defined to show why today's talent responds more often to authentic inspiration and trust.

The foundation of trust flows into the servant leader behavior in Chapter 15.

Finally, Chapter 16 connects servant leaders who create a multiplication effect rather than a diminishing, micro-management effect.

Each of these sections include a case history of how the workplace was transformed into a game-time performance center; how a win-win culture was created; how supervisors were transformed into coaches; and how employees' mindsets were transformed, freeing them to become high-performing Industrial Athletes.

MAKING THE TRANSFORMATION: THE FOUR QUESTIONS

As you read the remainder of this book, we invite you to reflect on and consider your own experiences within your organization. Ask these questions:

- **Workplace Experience:**
  Are we meeting our performance goals as an organization?
- **Culture Experience:**
  Is our culture an "I want to be here" culture, or is underlying conflict preventing a healthy environment where people can flourish?
- **Employee Experience:**
  Is our employee experience one that supports team members to give feedback and perform at their best for the good of the team?
- **Management Experience:**
  Are managers coaching with clarity and trust so that we have a healthy culture to achieve our performance results?

We invite you on this journey to improve your performance, both personally and organizationally. Identify what needs to change. Transform your workplace into a performance center, your tug-of-war culture into a win-win culture, your one-dimensional employees into Industrial Athletes and your bosses into coaches through this Industrial Athlete Operating System framework.

PART 1:
FROM WORKPLACE TO PERFORMANCE CENTER

"When they start the game, they don't yell, 'Work ball.' They say, 'Play ball.'" [11]

–Willie Stargell

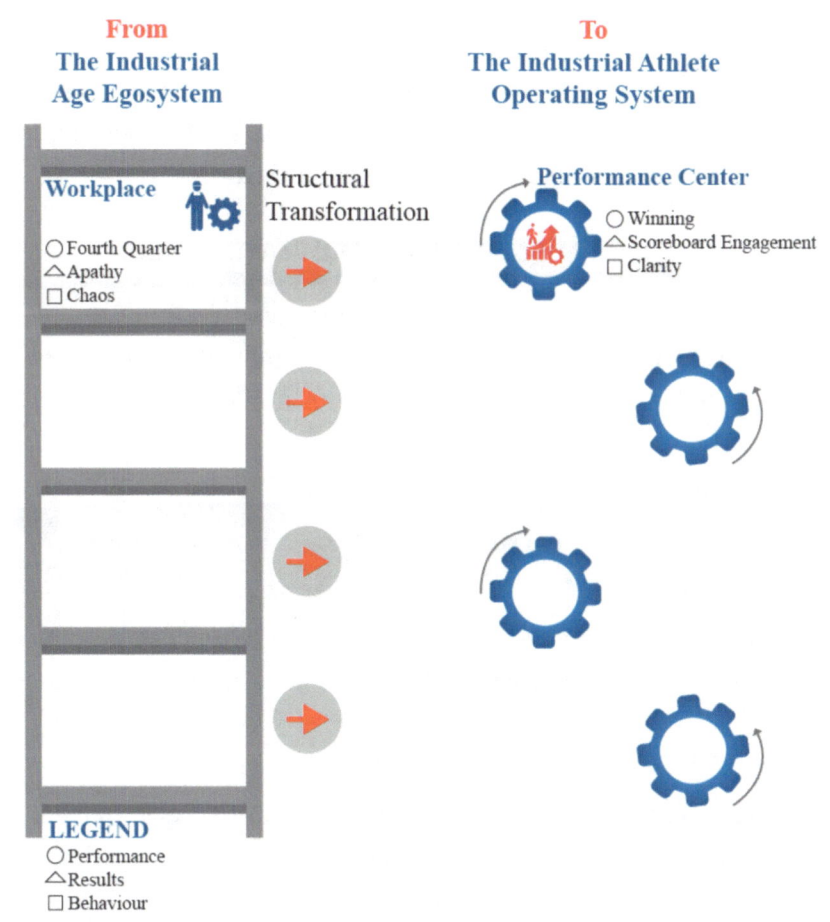

Figure 7: Workplace Transformation

Why are more sales in business made at the end of the month? Why are more points scored in the last two minutes of a ball game than at any other time? There is a sense of urgency. People see the scoreboard and the clock ticking down. Athletes know what they must do to reach a specific score before time runs out. They may feel the pressure as the clock dwindles toward zero, moving them into the psychological performance zone.

The rules, boundaries, and goals are clearly defined in sports, and players know their place and what is expected. The clock and the scoreboard make the game compelling for both players and fans. Likewise, turning a workplace into a performance center clarifies and creates full engagement and high-performance opportunities. The life of a high school football coach illustrates how this is accomplished.

FROM THE STREETS TO THE PLAYING FIELD

Ted Ginn Sr. has a history of turning low performers into high performers. Although Ginn has won state championships as a head high school football coach and has put more than 300 kids into Division 1 college, his chief focus is "Winning Lives."

He says,

"When you graduate kids, you win, but you dominate when you help them get employed, enlist, or enroll."

Football is simply the structure he uses to help young people find a way out of their challenging urban neighborhoods to make a difference.

The Streets

Ginn started as a volunteer assistant football coach and full-time uniformed security guard at Cleveland Glenville High School.[12] After 20 years as an assistant coach, Ginn became head coach in 1997. To be successful, he had to get out into the neighborhoods and find out what his future players were doing.

Ginn's mission included taking kids off the streets, where it is chaotic. They have shootings outside their houses, the rules are unclear, and it is not always policed. There is little guidance, and there is no way to keep the kids focused. They have no structure, cannot learn, and are traumatized. With their troubled lifestyle and lack of structure, the kids' brains are not functioning at full capacity, and they struggle in the school system. They are heading down a dead-end road with no hope of a future.

The Field of Performance

Ginn's program started by taking the young kids and putting them out on the playing field. The coaches would teach them their roles and goals and let them get started–and suddenly, they were learning. The very thing they could not do sitting in a classroom they could do on a playing field. Being on the playing field allowed them to progress faster because of the clarity of the field with boundaries, end zones, the scoreboard, and accountability.

Ginn's kids can learn on the playing field because it is a performance center, which differs from the streets. They are motivated to put more points on the scoreboard, and they have a competitive fire. Things happen quickly and all around them during the game, but they are learning to apply their brains. There are yardage markers on the field, touchdown markers, goalposts, rules, and referees. They obey the rules and listen to their coaches and the officials.

In 1999, Glenville became the first Cleveland public school to qualify for the state football playoffs. The Turboloaders made it to the playoffs eleven times in 12 years (1999 to 2010).[13]

THE EARNING IS IN THE LEARNING

Too often, our workplaces do not have the structure to motivate people to become high performers. A workplace is often a place of chaos with uncertainty and a lack of clarity. Harris Interactive surveyed 11,045 adult U.S. workers and found that only 12 percent of employees know their organization's key measures of success and how to keep score. The workers are unclear about where the organization is headed or its highest objectives. This lack of visual scorekeeping has created dismal results.

Imagine coaching a hockey team, but less than 20 percent of the players know which way their goal is. They would all be skating in different directions! The team does not win when people are caught up in the chaos of random activity; they win when players put more points on the scoreboard than the competition.

Figure 8 lists how a workplace differs from a performance center.

Workplace	Performance Center
Chaotic	Clarity
Static	Dynamic
Activity Focused	Action and result-focused
Work driven	Performance-driven
Reactive	Proactive
Fear of Failure	Fail Forward
Production alone	Production and potential
Stagnation	Growth
Every moment focused on the production	Gametime, training, and timeouts

Figure 8: Comparing Workplace to Performance Center

CHAPTER 5:
FROM CHAOS TO CLARITY

"Success is when vision meets reality."

—Mark Lamoncha

Now that we have overviewed the difference between a workplace and a performance center, we will look at the first step in making the transformation from chaos to clarity as smooth as possible, as shown in Figure 9.

Humtown transformed into a performance center after dropping from 226 employees to 17. Our performance was lacking because we were already in a marginalized business at the lower end of the spectrum. At that time, our employee healthcare costs were greater than our raw material costs. It was chaotic as we experienced a staff turnover as high as 75 percent. Labor costs rose as high as 50 percent because of inefficiencies.

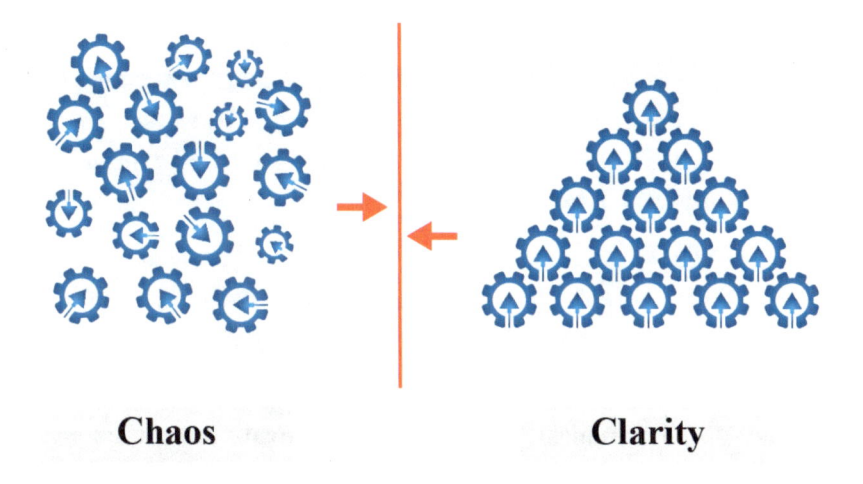

Chaos   **Clarity**

Figure 9: From Chaos to Clarity

To facilitate a place where Industrial Athletes could thrive, we shifted from the unengaging, uninspiring typical just-show-up workplace to an industrial performance center. We focused on developing a new mission, values, and priorities to embrace real-time feedback using technology with rewards.

A DEFINING MOMENT: INTRO TO VISUAL EARNINGS™

Mark recalls,

"In 2008, our company was negatively impacted during the auto industry crisis that led to a great recession. When General Motors, Chrysler, and other manufacturers went bankrupt, I feared we would also go bankrupt. I felt like we would never recover. We needed a new mindset and toolset to transform our company if we were going to survive.

I felt hopeless due to the magnitude of the calamity. So, I decided to buy a lottery ticket, thinking we might win enough money to keep us on our feet. Unfortunately, the lottery ticket did not produce the millions I hoped for, so I decided to buy another ticket.

At the time, I was reminded of an idea that James Lincoln from Lincoln Electric had. Lincoln had been bankrupt until he had the idea to turn Lincoln Electric around using an incentive system. This idea was what saved Lincoln Electric. I asked myself, 'What would James Lincoln do today?'

That night, I prayed for an idea like the one that came to Lincoln. When I woke up the following morning, I had a divine idea of a visual, real-time earning system that measures and shows team members their productivity rate."

The Visual Earnings™ System became a real-time earning system technology that engages team members through data science and gamification to increase productivity when performing repetitive, measurable tasks.

This VES earned Humtown the 2020 Manufacturing Leadership Award in the Engineering and Production Technology Leadership category from the National Association of Manufacturers alongside IBM, General Motors, and Peterbilt. Higher output translates to a higher earnings rate, updated every machine cycle, and displayed in real-time on a user interface.

The idea of the VES inspired us to transform our workplace into a performance center; to do that, we had to create clarity, so we developed a new mission, a new vision, and new priorities. Our team members began to feel like the real winners–knowing what they had to do to win, learning how to keep score, and knowing when we would check in to increase performance.

Once trained as a pilot, Mark compares an organization to an airplane. The transformation from a workplace to a performance center is like the transformation from a blimp to an F-15. It accelerates faster, reaches top speeds, and achieves more victories. It provides clarity and motivation and focuses energy on keeping team members on track. The four forces of flight–lift, thrust, drag, and weight–act together on the aircraft. Controlling those forces allows the pilot to maneuver the airplane and makes flight possible. In a similar way, forming a compelling vision is the first strategic step toward a successful flight for an organization.

Our MVP playbook process aligns the organization's core purpose with the strategies and behaviors needed for successful outcomes. The process follows the acronym MVP, which stands for Mission, Vision, and Priorities.

Mission

A mission is our clear purpose for existing. It is our *why*! If we are going on a trip, we need to know our reason for going. Is it for business, to see family, or for a vacation? It is essential that everyone involved rally around our mission.

Vision

A vision statement is a picture of the preferred future. It is comparable to the destination of our trip. Our vision statement shows our stakeholders what the world will look like if they fulfill our mission. The vision statement is aspirational and gives hope for all team members to rally around.

Priorities

Priorities are broad, long-term aims that define the fulfillment of the vision. How will we know if we had a successful trip? The answer lies in our priorities: Did we accomplish what we intended?

CHAPTER 5: FROM CHAOS TO CLARITY

Your Playbook: How You Can Make the Transformation

Your mission, vision, and priorities are a starting point for creating clarity. Questions to consider when creating clarity.

1. Are your mission, vision, and priorities relevant?

2. Do your team members know what the MVP Playbook includes to distinguish and align concepts?

3. **Mission** – Ask your team: Is our mission still relevant? Are the people in our organization infused with purpose by our mission? If not, how should we update our mission statement to achieve greater engagement?

4. **Vision** – When team members have clarity, you have taken the first step to create a fully engaged team.

5. **Priorities** – If we only accomplish two or three things in the next three to five years and we do nothing else, what would those two or three things be? Identify the key areas of focus that will help fulfill your vision. If there are too many, some may not be a priority. You will then know your priorities.

Notes
_____
_____
_____
_____
_____
_____

CHAPTER 6:
FROM APATHY TO ENGAGEMENT

"When people are financially invested, they want a return. When people are emotionally invested, they want to contribute."

–Simon Sinek

Building on our flight analogy from the MVP playbook, it is time to get this plane off the ground and move toward our destination by creating engagement.

Real-time feedback is in keeping with the psychology of flow or the psychology of the performance zone. The performance zone is created when a person is completely focused and fully engaged in an activity. Being in this state of mind enables a person to perform at their peak because they clearly understand their goals and required activities as they receive immediate feedback.

HOW VISUAL EARNINGS™ ENHANCED ENGAGEMENT

VES is not only helping Humtown to thrive as a business but is also addressing the major societal issue of disengagement. When people are disengaged, it affects more than their work, it also affects their personal lives. People may become discouraged and depressed, causing personal, family, and community problems. When people are actively engaged, they are more productive at work, and they can lead a better life outside of work, helping the family and the community.

With the Visual Earnings™ System operating on individual scoreboards, payroll is visible, cycle to cycle, so that the Industrial Athlete can make changes in real-time, and the outcomes are instant. Industrial Athletes are plugged in instantaneously, as with the stock market, to see how they affect a change in their wages. This helps to keep team members constantly engaged.

Engaging our whole self in the activity while receiving real-time feedback from the scoreboard can help us achieve optimal performance. In a split second, we can look at the scoreboard, determine our productivity level, and decide what to do next.

Millennials or Generation Zs like to see their feedback as a score on the screen like in a video game. This instant response rewards them with greater meaning of their intentional actions so that they find fulfillment in their work.

The key engagement factor that has driven Humtown's success involves the reason people work: to make money. We wanted to show our workers the strong connection between their productivity on a machine and the money they make per hour.[14] That's why we conducted a study of incentive plans at other companies around the country. We determined that some good plans were being used, but they were often complex or involved delayed payoffs (some a year later).

We intuitively knew that increased engagement would require an incentive plan that provided instant gratification. We decided to incentivize factory performance by converting the labor portion of the job to a visual earning rate in real-time, empowering team members to take ownership of their earnings by truly engaging in their tasks. The technology increases earnings for workers by involving them to produce at an elevated level in a game-like environment.

This is the matrix the Industrial Athletes see on their screens as they reach various percentage points:

175% over quoted rate = Fireworks
250% over quoted rate = Flames
275% over quoted rate = Flames with their picture
300% over quoted rate = Nuclear bomb

CHAPTER 6: FROM APATHY TO ENGAGEMENT 51

Figure 10 illustrates what the Visual Earnings™ System at each workstation looks like.

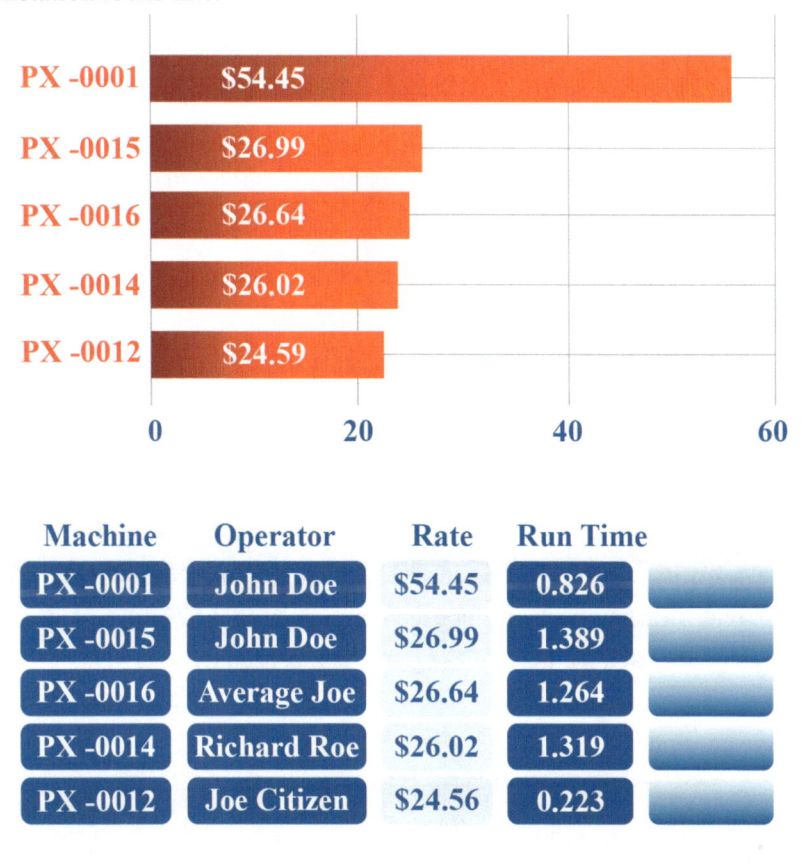

Machine	Operator	Rate	Run Time
PX -0001	John Doe	$54.45	0.826
PX -0015	John Doe	$26.99	1.389
PX -0016	Average Joe	$26.64	1.264
PX -0014	Richard Roe	$26.02	1.319
PX -0012	Joe Citizen	$24.56	0.223

Figure 10: Visual Earnings ™ System Gamification

Each team member has a workstation as if they are in business for themselves, without all the other headaches that come with owning a business. They know what activities need to be performed to increase their score and achieve their desired outcomes. When team members log in and run their first cycle, they immediately know how much the combination of their skills, abilities, and performance will reward them.

Dave Arthurs, a senior software engineer and part of the brains behind the Visual Earnings™ System, explains some of the data science and gamification on the screens:

"It is kind of like that game you would play at a fair when you squirt water at a balloon and the first one to pop their balloon wins. You see the gauge rising to the top and it adds an element of friendly competition.

Each job has a rate, and that rate is determined by how many pieces can be made within an hour. If they're logged in for an hour and they meet the quota, then they earn the standard rate. If it only takes them half an hour, they get double the rate. Seeing their pay rate in a real time system which incentivizes the process makes it more fun."

This system is relatively easy for team members to use and understand. The gamification puts the Industrial Athletes into a competition. Games with real-time feedback produce a dopamine hit in the brain, and the player keeps going back for more if the game is incentivized.

Dave continues:

"The screen resembles a top 10 list that you would see at a bowling alley, where everyone is vying for a top spot. It is very motivating because many people watch that Top 10 and try to outdo their friends."

All our quality information is delivered to team members on the app on their own VES devices. Their dashboard shows them the process sheet and how the part should be made. If they make it wrong, they see their rate drop because they must log their scrap. They learn that if they make a mistake with the quality of a part, they must not repeat the mistake because it immediately negatively impacts their rate. Rather, they must stop and make a new one.

We built a quality alert into the patented software that goes into the Siemens PLC and stops the machine. Quality alerts in most companies are usually discovered after the fact and emailed or put up on the bulletin board. But in this case, we have a real-time, integrated manufacturing 4.0 stop-point to avoid making the same mistake twice.

Because we believe that the integrity of the person creates the integrity of the product, every person must swipe their badge to operate a machine. If they are not certified/approved, the software is engineered to keep the machine from operating. These systems protect us on a quality basis, and they also protect us on a safety basis.

Team members watch their earning rate increase in real-time. Some team members increased their performance by over 400 percent! They earned more, and Humtown's company profits increased accordingly.

Because gamification is an intricate part of a performance center, we created a simulation game called Gopher Gold™ that is used in the interview process. Our HR coach competes with a prospective team member during the interview to see who can score the most points during a set period by whacking the gopher. This is the first window into whether the person has the competitive nature it takes to succeed as an Industrial Athlete. If we see that sparkle in their eye, they will probably fit well within the VES environment.

Your Playbook: How You Can Make the Transformation

Now is the time to check your own scoreboard. People may disengage when they don't know the score.
To move from apathy to engagement, consider these questions:

1. Do you have a measurable engagement survey or tool that will help you to discover and evaluate what your team members need to become more engaged and productive?

2. Do you have a method to quantify your team members' level of engagement?

3. How can you determine if team members are coming to work fully engaged and excited because they control their performance?

4. Does everyone know what they need to achieve their goals?

5. Do people meet regularly to review and evaluate their performance compared to the standards?

Notes
_____
_____
_____
_____
_____

CHAPTER 7:
FROM FOURTH-QUARTER FAILURE TO A WINNING SCOREBOARD

"I've always craved winning. It's just easier in sports because there's a scoreboard."

–Sam Hunt

A scoreboard is like a GPS flight instrument for a pilot. It is a way to track performance and let us know if we are on target. It allows us to make clearer decisions because it provides real-time intelligence. We can always look at the instrument panel in times of uncertainty. The numbers will not lie.

Performance scoreboards can be for the individual, the team, or the organization. **Nothing else we have found compares to the motivation of a scoreboard with real-time incentives**. When people keep score, team members respond positively and perform differently. Take a moment and think about it. What if you remove the scoreboard from a football game? What would happen? Would it make the game less exciting?

For the scoreboard to be successful, it should be straightforward, always visible to the team, and instantly show whether your team members are progressing toward the goals. This will promote and reward positive activity through clear expectations. Performance scoreboards have the power to transform an organization's culture from one that is ambiguous to one that is high performing.

Scoreboards, more than anything else, were the catalyst that brought about every other transformation. Our Industrial Athletes use the proprietary **Visual Earnings™ System** to know how they perform at every moment. It also helps the leadership know how they are performing as a group based on everyone's collective performance. Performance results and scoreboard measures help coaches and industrial athletes experience movement towards the desired direction.

HOW VISUAL EARNINGS™ CREATED A WINNING SCOREBOARD

Measuring and showing team members their productivity through effective gamification increased pay rates. All stakeholders benefited from the system, and the team members' earnings and company profits went up. Humtown saw sustained increases in productivity from 70 percent up to 1,000 percent!

The data is updated every machine cycle and displayed in real-time on their user interface. Industrial Athletes constantly sharpen their skill set, abilities, and performance results.

Humtown used to run 24 hours a day in four shifts. The different shifts would point fingers and blame others if something went wrong. There was no synergy. Mark realized the teams needed to act like hockey players, communicating between shift changes to keep everyone fully in the performance zone, but that was not happening.

As part of the solution, we changed from four eight8-hour shifts per day, six or sometimes seven days a week, to a work schedule of six hours a day, six days a week.[15] We accomplished more during the new six-hour shifts than during the long ones.

Sheri Lamoncha believes that the 6-hour shifts are one of the most impactful positive changes that have been made through the **Visual Earnings™** development. She says,

> "The Industrial Athletes can hit it and hit it hard and remain in a good frame of mind for six hours, but beyond that, it becomes overly stressful. The shorter shifts are less stressful because the people have less cortisol running through them, which allows them to get more done for the time they are there and live healthier, more productive lives."

We first used the Visual Earnings™ System on a project that involved making cores for the front engine cover for Chrysler minivans. At the time, we produced an average of 400 pieces in an eight-hour shift. Following

CHAPTER 7: FROM FOURTH-QUARTER FAILURE TO WINNING SCOREBOARD   57

the implementation of the Visual Earnings™ System, our productivity jumped approximately 400 percent, and as a result, we were able to create up to 14,140 items in just six hours.

Before the Visual Earnings™ System, 152 employees generated $247,000 weekly in manufacturing sales. After implementing the Visual Earnings™ System, we generated more than $300,000 weekly with 26 Industrial Athletes. Since implementing the new system, we have saved millions of dollars in lost productivity.

When Industrial Athletes have the unlimited potential to earn based on performance rather than a fixed hourly wage, the organizational performance and revenue have the ability to increase substantially. For example, The Visual Earnings™ System Scoreboard created a net turnaround of $19 million in Humtown's first 10 years of using it.

Humtown's transformation came from solving a basic problem: how to improve the company's inefficiencies. Mark realized that people want to see validation of the value they are hired for in real-time.

VISUAL EARNINGS™ PRODUCED PHENOMENAL RESULTS

Early application of the Visual Earnings™ System produced earnings increase of 175% for the hourly rate and an increase of 615% in monthly production sales per worker. Figure 11 demonstrates how much of an effect a scoreboard may have on the performance of individuals.

	Before	After	% Change
Worker hourly earning rate average	$8.00	$22.00	175%
Monthly production sales per worker	$60,894	$435,431	615%
Direct labor costs (% of COS)	20.20%	10.40%	-49%
Healthcare costs (% of COS)	6.80%	1.46%	-78%
Net profit (% of revenue)	-5%	14%	1890%

Figure 11: Visual Earnings™ Change

Your Playbook: How You Can Make the Transformation

A compelling scoreboard tells your team members where they are and where they need to be. Data is vital to acting. When team members themselves are keeping score, they tend to understand the connection between their performance and reaching their goal, and this changes the level at which they play. When everyone on the team can see the score, the level of play increases because they can see what's working and what modifications are needed. Let's have a look at the ways in which you may help motivate the members of your team to take action by using their own scoreboards.

Ask yourself these questions.

1. How can you move your team from apathy to engagement so that team members can quickly determine whether or not they are winning?

2. How visible is the scoreboard, and does it increase team members focus on the task?

3. How can you creatively use scoreboards to advance engagement and higher performance?

Notes

_____
_____
_____
_____
_____

PART 1
CONCLUSION

Many people naturally perform better in an exciting performance center rather than a mundane workspace. By transforming your workplace from chaos to clarity, engagement becomes the prevalent theme within the environment. A visual scoreboard in the form of a G.A.M.E. plan may fully engage your team members, enabling them to take more control of the outcomes. That is when your organization could transition from fourth-quarter failure to winning every day.

The key to all this is really a scoreboard. And we know that a scoreboard is really what attracts people, right? It engages us. The GAME is on!

- **G** = Goal clarity. Does everyone know the most important goals?
- **A** = Action steps or activities that tie to the goals. Does everyone know what action steps need to be taken to achieve the goals?
- **M** is a Measurable scoreboard. Do you have a measurable scoreboard everyone can see?
- **E** is an Evaluation Calendar used to check in for continuous improvement. Do you have an evaluation calendar that you revisit regularly to measure success?

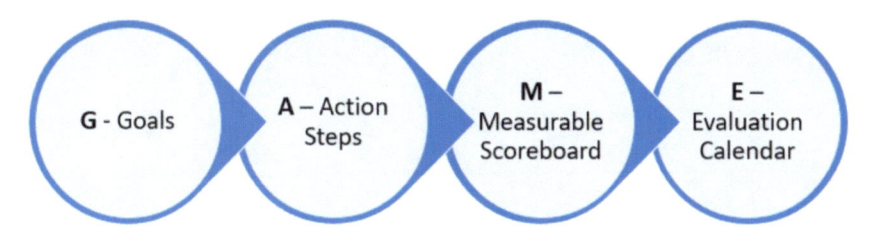

Figure 12: GAME Plan

PART 2:
FROM A TUG-OF-WAR TO A WIN-WIN CULTURE

"Culture Eats Strategy for Breakfast."

–Peter Drucker

From
The Industrial Age Egosystem

To
The Industrial Athlete Operating System

Workplace
- ◯ Fourth Quarter
- △ Apathy
- ☐ Chaos

Structural Transformation ➡

Performance Center
- ◯ Winning
- △ Scoreboard Engagement
- ☐ Clarity

Tug-of-War Culture
- ◯ Downward Spiral
- △ Subtle Sabotage
- ☐ Us vs. Them

Social Transformation ➡

Win-Win Culture
- ◯ Upward Spiral
- △ Trusted Teamwork
- ☐ Win -Win

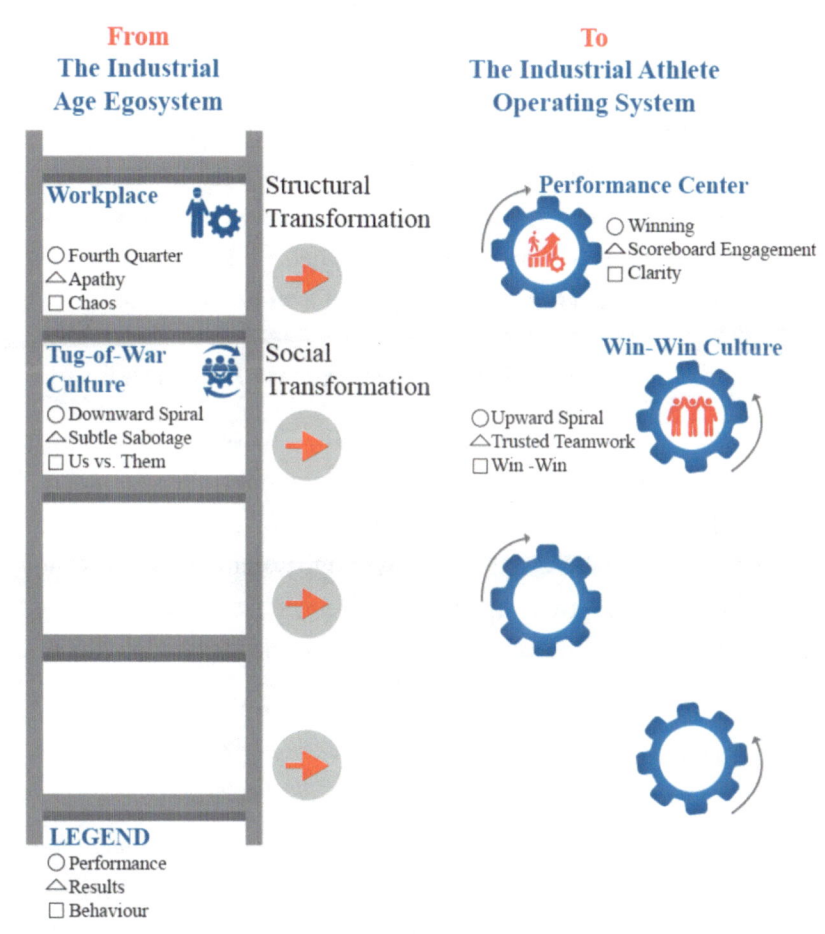

LEGEND
- ◯ Performance
- △ Results
- ☐ Behaviour

Figure 13: Cultural Transformation Defined

In Part 2, Culture Transformation changes the direction of the spiral from the subtle sabotage caused by "us vs. them" to "trusted teamwork," resulting in a win-win environment.

- In a tug-of-war culture, people selfishly seek status at the expense of the collective results of the organization.
- In a win-win culture, people support and replenish each other so that everyone wins.

Business culture is often considered an invisible, emotional part of the organization that leaders do not have to address, so it should be no surprise that 80 percent of employees believe that their organization's culture needs to change.

Imagine taking people from "I must be at work" to "I cannot wait to get to work to enjoy and perform." When we get to that point, we could have a level of engagement that drives success and fulfillment in ways we have not known before. That is also when we know that we have crossed the bridge from a tug-of-war culture to a win-win culture.

THE HEAVEN AND HELL OF A CULTURE

When functioning as a healthy win-win culture, the social environment can feel like heaven to its members. People want to be there, feel like they have purpose, and trust each other. However, it can feel like hell when a culture is a tug-of-war egosystem. This can result in team member health problems, high absenteeism, and low engagement.

To tell the difference, let us look at the story of the long and short spoons.

One day, a woman conversed with the Lord and said, "Lord, I would like to know what Heaven and Hell are like."

The Lord led the woman to two doors. He opened one of the doors and the woman looked in. In the middle of the room was a large round table. In the middle of the table was a large bowl of soup which smelled delicious and made the woman's mouth water.

The people sitting around the table were thin and sickly. They appeared to be famished. They were holding spoons with exceptionally long handles. Each found it possible to reach into the bowl of soup and take a spoonful, but because the handle was longer than their arms, they could not get the spoons back into their mouths. The woman shuddered at the sight of their misery and suffering. The Lord said, "You have seen what it is like to experience hell." [16]

They went to the next room and opened the door; it looked the same as the first one. The bowl of soup on the large round table made the woman's mouth water. The people were equipped with the same long-handled spoons, but those people were well nourished and plump, laughing and talking. The Lord said, "You have seen what it is like to experience heaven." [17]

The woman said, "I do not understand. Both rooms are the same, yet one is full of misery, and the other is filled with happiness."

"It is simple," said the Lord. "It requires the right attitude. In the heavenly room, they are a team and have learned to feed each other. In the other room, they only think of themselves, resulting in famine."

In an egosystem, employees compete against each other to climb the corporate ladder instead of teaming together. People are tugging and at war with one another rather than working together. With no psychological safety, people unintentionally sabotage production and performance.

On the other hand, a win-win culture values nurturing and investing in stakeholders who support and replenish one another. Shifting an organization's culture to an ecosystem provides a supportive environment for the Industrial Athlete and their organization to perform at a peak level.

Figure 14 details the differences between a tug-of-war culture and a win-win culture.

Tug-of-War Egosystem	Win-Win Culture
Self- Interest	Shared Interest
I must be here	I get to be here
Scarcity	Abundance
Corporate Ladder	Everyone Matters
Shareholders	All Stakeholders
What is in it for me?	How can I serve 'we'?
Hierarchy	Independent Network

Figure 14: Tug-of-War vs. Win-Win Culture

CHAPTER 8:
FROM US VS. THEM TO WIN-WIN

"You can have anything in life that you want if you will just help other people get what they want."

–Zig Ziglar

Once your workplace and culture are transformed, your employees will be more willing to engage their heads, hands, and hearts. In this chapter we will see how Humtown was transformed into a place where all stakeholders benefited.

For the first 30 years, we did things the same way, producing tug-of-war ego battles. Every moment was focused on production and putting out fires, and everyone was continually drained. As for our culture, we did not have time to work on it or to nurture our team members. This created a workforce that felt they *had* to be there rather than wanting to be there.

Even though Mark owned the company, he felt like he *had* to get up and go to work; he did not *want* to.

Mark says,

"I was like the person in the joke where the mother says to her son,

"You need to get up and go to work."

He says, "Give me two good reasons."

She says, "Number one, you are 42 years old, and number two, you are the company's president."

We found that it is not just the employees who did not want to get up and go to work in the morning; the owners and leaders did not want to either. And who can blame them when team members worked against each other, were demotivated, and there was a power struggle between management and employees This lack of engagement was not unique to Humtown, either.

Brandon relays a story he heard from one of his clients:

"The press on a machine broke, so the machine operator sat down and started reading the newspaper. A new guy in maintenance ran over to repair it and the guy reading the paper asked, 'Why would you do that?'"

It made no difference to the machine operator if the press stayed broken. He would get paid his hourly rate to read the paper while his machine stood idle, not producing anything. This story reinforced Humtown's belief that, until machine operators are given the capacity to determine their own rate, they will not care about downtime because it affects the company, not them.

A WIN-WIN CREATES THE WILL TO WIN

Tim recalls,

"I went to Chicago and learned to diagnose culture in depth from Robert Cooke of Human Synergistics. Cooke defined culture as shared values and beliefs that lead to behavioral norms that guide the way members of an organization approach their work."

Every organization has one of three mindsets and behavior patterns that make up its culture: win-win, win-lose, or lose-win. Culture comprises many shared agreements; some are consciously shared agreements, and some are unconscious. Any agreement can have one of those three outcomes. When we take all the conscious and unconscious agreements and put them together, we have an overarching theme within an organization. That overarching theme is either win-win, win-lose, or lose-win. However, every win-lose or lose-win will become a lose-lose culture.[18]

Figure 15: Culture Spectrum

A win-win culture is characterized by people who have confidence. They are vibrant and excited about their work. They are interacting with joy; they *want* to be there. Conversely, a culture that is either lose-win or win-lose identifies people who feel that they *must* be there but do not *want* to. Their hands and heads are in the game, not their hearts.

A win-win culture engages the whole being. The heart is *motivating* the energy. The head is *thinking* to process information and make decisions. The hands are *doing*–typing on the computer, taking a call, making it to the next meeting on time. In other words, these integrated connections invigorate a win-win culture that fuels greater productivity.

A DEFINING MOMENT:
HOW VES HELPED TO CREATE A WIN-WIN CULTURE

The Visual Earnings™ System became a helpful leadership tool that set a new tone to enhance Humtown's performance and culture. We changed our way of looking at things. We needed a cultural transformation. We went from making the company about *me* to making it about *we*. Even though the VES was more of a technological concept, a new mindset and heart transformation developed because of Mark's defining moment with how to help the Visual Earnings™ create a win-win.

Mark shares his epiphany:

"My dad used to say, 'If people only knew how much a minute cost to the company.'

My response after studying what he said was, "What mattered to them was not how much a minute cost the company, but how much a minute cost them personally."

Mine was a kind of radical way of thinking. I am glad my dad thought about the cost, but I know team members do not have time to be concerned about the company's percentages and rates. They care more about how much a minute costs them than how much it costs the company. Therefore, we had to take numbers and percentages that meant a lot to the company and transform them into numbers that meant a lot to the team members for their workstations.

This was diametrically opposed to the old way we communicated with them. Their hourly rate is important if they come to work only to make money. The epiphany I had was to amplify the number that they cared about. My production staff did not want to hear me ranting about how we needed to increase our production while their rate stayed the same. THEY CARED A LOT MORE when I linked their hourly rate to their production!"

The Visual Earnings™ System uses a simple calculation to determine an Industrial Athlete's earnings. For example, if they make ten parts per hour, they earn $10. If they make twenty parts per hour, they earn $20. Sometimes the job would require ten parts per hour, but team members made fifty. Then, they would shift their earnings from $10 to $50 per hour. Every work cycle, the team member instantly sees the pay rate on a computer screen. The average hourly pay rate reached more than $46 per hour. As represented in Figure 16, one of Humtown's Industrial Athletes ran a job at a 1,031 percent rate, so he made $103.10 per hour. Humtown made $2,062.00 to cover its costs and profit.

How is that for a win-win?!

CHAPTER 8: FROM US VS. THEM TO WIN-WIN

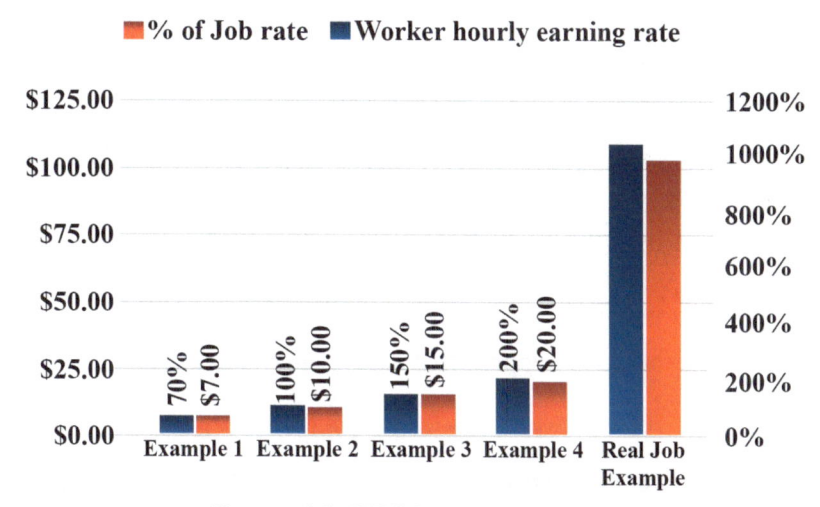

Figure 16: VES Percentage Chart

Creating a win-win culture requires transformation from the inside out. For us, it began when Mark had an epiphany that every stakeholder is important. After doing things the "old way" for 30 years, it was time for a breakthrough. The breakthrough came in the realization that we needed to care about which numbers were most important to our team members, and partner with them rather than working against them.

Your Playbook: How You Can Make the Transformation

A win-win culture enables team members and the organization to execute strategic initiatives, accomplish goals, and fulfill the mission. Ask yourself these questions when developing a win-win culture.

1. Do people have the opportunity to set their own goals?

2. Do they have the opportunity to determine their own production level and pay level?

3. Do people feel like they have appropriate working conditions?

4. Are people recognized and appreciated for work well done?

5. Is there a chance for promotion and growth in the organization?

Notes
_____
_____
_____
_____
_____

CHAPTER 9:
FROM SUBTLE SABOTAGE TO TRUSTED TEAMWORK

"In a high-trust relationship, you can say the wrong thing, and people will still get your meaning. In a low-trust relationship, you can be very measured, even precise, and they'll still misinterpret you."
–Stephen M.R. Covey

Can a single conflict between just two individuals make a difference in an organization's culture? Yes. Two team members who have an unresolved conflict can divide the entire team and disrupt the organizational culture. We will discover how subtle sabotage can damage any organization, while trusted teamwork is an invaluable asset.

Whenever an unresolved conflict exists between parties, each person's brain tries to resolve it in their own way. If conflict is not addressed in a meeting, it is frequently addressed elsewhere. If the individuals do not resolve the issues, they force others to choose sides, drawing them into the argument. This is the beginning of the often-unconscious process of building allies or a network of allies that can subtly sabotage the organization's goals.

Imagine a team member who does not speak to a coworker because of an unresolved conflict. After the meeting, this team member may talk with other team members about how they feel; this is "the meeting after the meeting" at the water cooler. These conversations can turn team members against one another as each listener chooses someone with whom to side.

When a team member works against the leader's vision and goals, the leader often feels the undercurrent. The situation worsens when the leader tells other people about it without addressing the person concerned. The leader may also choose to share with others in leadership, people they trust more. In doing so, they begin to build their own team of allies as shown in Figure 17. Neither party realizes they are building allies; they simply feel they are working through the conflict by talking about it.

Figure 17: Tug-of-War Culture

Two opposing teams are formed in these two separate conversations, turning people against each other. What was once an impasse between two people has now infected more people, creating allies in opposing teams. A tug-of-war egosystem subtly sabotages the organization's goals.

As these moments of subtle sabotage continue to happen, they can create a downward spiral in the organization's culture and negatively impact its profits.

THE SUBTLE IMPACT OF SUBTLE SABOTAGE

Mark recalls specific challenges.

"We would have industrial engineers come in and perform a time study to know how long a job should take for quoting purposes. Whenever the industrial engineer did a time study, he often raised the production rate, making it harder for the employees to make extra money. The company benefited from the employees' improvements and efficiency without rewarding them.

Unfortunately, the employees reverse-engineered ways to subtly sabotage the job to counteract the increase. They would intentionally stretch the project to deceive the industrial engineers.

CHAPTER 9: FROM SUBTLE SABOTAGE TO TRUSTED TEAMWORK

It created ego battles that ended in a tug-of-war lose-lose situation."

The management team was seen as the enemy because the employees were expected to work harder for the same pay. Trust was depleted. The employees and the engineer repelled one another.

Zach, who is a coach at Humtown, recalls,

"When Mark started with the VES, people were very unclear about what he was doing. There was a lot of mistrust; it was not easy for Mark. Many people were suspicious that Mark was just trying to get more money from them, get them to work harder, and pay them less, when, in fact, it was the complete opposite."

In hindsight, we realize that our team members' potential was locked in Pay-Rate Jail™. Now, it has been released through our Visual Earnings™ System.

This Pay-Rate Jail™ setting did not create trust, but rather, subtle sabotage among team members. No one benefited when the industrial engineer did his time studies only to have the production crew silently sabotage his engineering skills. It kept us distracted and our business constricted.

However, once we were equipped with this understanding, we could move toward building trust.

MOVING TO TRUST AND PSYCHOLOGICAL SAFETY

Leaders set the tone that will form the underlying attitudes of the culture. In other words, a leader needs to be less like a thermometer and more like a thermostat. A thermometer only *tells* the temperature, but a thermostat *sets* the temperature. In this analogy, the temperature is the tone of the organization's culture, and the culture will suffer if the leaders react to the conflict without navigating it well. When leaders set the tone rather than reacting to what everyone else is doing, those in the organization can respond positively to the proactive leadership, and employee trust can increase.

We began to see our team members flourish rather than being locked up. Identifying how they could be more innovative to enhance their performance became the ultimate solution where everyone benefits, and a higher trust became more practical.

By measuring organizational culture, the invisible is visible and allows for setting a baseline and benchmark for improvement. According to Google's Project Aristotle, psychological safety is the #1 factor influencing team performance and success.

Rework.withgoogle.com describes psychological safety at work:

"In a team with high psychological safety, teammates feel safe to take risks around their team members. They feel confident that no team member will embarrass or punish anyone for admitting a mistake, asking a question, or offering a new idea."

One day, when Mark and his friend and fellow business owner Sam Shinko were driving together, Sam told Mark a story of when he worked at Urick Foundry. Sam pitched an idea to his boss who did not buy into the idea, but he did not discount or discredit it either. Rather, he allowed Sam to try the new idea. When he failed, his boss asked,

"What did you learn from that?"

There are no failures but rather a FAIL, which is an acronym for First Attempt in Learning. The world's greatest lessons come from failing forward. Sam learned through trying, which is one of the greatest educational opportunities. What Sam learned through the FAIL acronym helped him become the owner and president of his own foundry company.

Mark says,

"Unfortunately, most leaders do not see the classroom of failure as the greatest learning arena. If we make someone feel bad for losing money or time, we miss the opportunity to see the incident as an educational opportunity. They will lock up their potential at that moment and may never release it again."

In his *Harvard Business Review* article called "The Neuroscience of Trust," Paul Zak states that team members in high-trust organizations are more productive and have more energy at work. High-trust team members collaborate better with their colleagues and stay with their employers longer. Compared with people at low-trust companies, people at high-trust companies report 74 percent less stress and 106 percent more energy when working.[19]

A climate of trust grows when relationships are intentionally built and transparency is demonstrated. Trust is further established when everyone's voice is valued, compensation is fair and equitable, and win-win methods for conflict resolution are in place. The climate of trust decreases when there is a lack of transparency and people feel that their voices do not count.

Humtown recognizes that a business and the sum of their team members are the same. When team members win, the business wins. VES was specifically designed to provide a counter-intuitive outcome; as the worker earns more, the company earns more.

We recommend using a DISC personality profile from PeopleKeys. These profiles, available at https://peoplekeys.com/, have transformed the way we understand and interact with one another. By delving into everyone's unique working style, we've unlocked a level of trust and cohesion that has elevated our performance.

With the help of DISC, we've come to appreciate the intricacies of communication styles, decision-making processes, and interaction preferences. This has led to smoother collaboration, enriched our leadership development initiatives, and enhanced our interpersonal dynamics.

Leaders set the tone for organizational success. With the right mindset, no one fails. Rather, every First Attempt in Learning (FAIL) is an opportunity for growth.

Your Playbook: How You Can Make the Transformation

A climate of belonging and trust develops when everyone feels safe to learn and contribute. This environment is effective when conflicts are resolved through win-win methods, where transparency and accountability are rewarded. What are ways to increase trust within your culture? Consider the following points.

1. Do we use a trust measurement tool to obtain feedback with all stakeholders to build trusting relationships?

2. Would the people of your organization say that there is a climate of transparency?

3. Do team members feel that leadership is approachable?

4. Team members that trust one another's intentions are in the best interest of each other and the team.

5. Team members willingly apologize to one another when needed.

6. Team members are able to learn from their mistakes.

Notes
_____
_____
_____
_____
_____

CHAPTER 10: FROM DOWNWARD SPIRAL TO UPWARD SYNERGY

"Momentum is an amazing thing when it is working in your favor."

–Simon Mignolet

A climate of trust is like a bank account where you deposit goodwill through good practices instead of depositing money. When people believe there is goodwill, they trust the intentions of leaders, which begins the upward synergy.

HOW HUMTOWN CAUGHT UPWARD SYNERGY

When Humtown set out to transform culture, we began with the people inside, but the transformation resonated beyond the company's walls. When we give people a reason to exist, it creates hope for everyone around them, resulting in upward synergy versus a downward spiral, as shown in Figure 18.

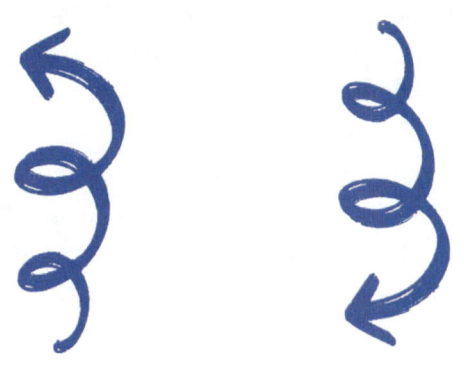

Figure 18: Upward Synergy vs. Downward Spiral

As the **Industrial Athlete Operating System** emerged, we began to see people differently. We no longer saw them as objects for our profit alone. Mark shifted his thinking from how to profit *despite* people, transitioning to how to profit *through* people.

Mark explains:

> *"To shift our culture at Humtown, we intentionally took a servant leadership approach with all stakeholders and internal customers as we once did with only our external customers."*

The VALYOU-ME-360 ™ cycle, represented in Figure 19, describes each stakeholder group with the acronym TEAMS. This acronym conveys our focus on increasing performance.

- **T**–TREASURE Team Members.
  First, we treasured our team members. What was once a secondary focus became primary.
- **E**–ESTEEM Economic Investors.
  We esteemed our economic investors and their vision to see the value in everyone.
- **A**–APPRECIATE Alliance Partners.
  We appreciate our partners, vendors, and suppliers. By appreciating each other, the company's appreciation grows along with the company's tangible financial value.
- **M**–MINISTER to the Marketplace.
  We have always valued our customers, but now we minister to the marketplace. Our team members realize that they are not working for Humtown but for our customers and other stakeholders.
- **S**–SERVE Society.
  We chose to serve the broader community and society. We serve our school systems, national associations, local police, fire departments, etc.

CHAPTER 10: FROM DOWNWARD SPIRAL TO UPWARD SYNERGY

Humtown was heading for bankruptcy, but valuing people made the difference in our recovery as a company. To build a high-trust, high-performance company and adhere to the stakeholder-centered model, we needed to get the process working from the inside out.

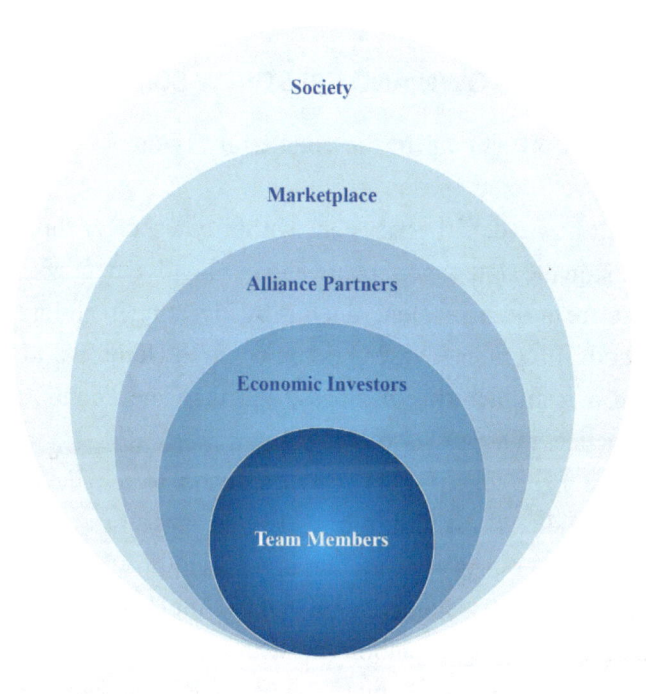

Figure 19: Inside Out ValYou Process

Following through on this process has increased our performance and profitability. All stakeholders have become sources and resources that nurture and replenish themselves, becoming a greater ecosystem.

Mark describes an instance where team members were invited to help problem-solve:

"Rather than just having top management make all the decisions, we gave our team members opportunities to solve more problems. For example, we flew our front-line team members to their headquarters when Tesla needed us for emergency work. The team was then able to develop and implement solutions."

Developing a high-trust ecosystem requires valuing, investing in, and cultivating a vast network of interdependent stakeholders. Mark was able to understand the value of the greater community beyond the scope of daily activities. This includes serving on the governor's state school board and assisting local schools.

HUMTOWN AND CRESTVIEW SCHOOLS

Humtown's investment in the community is the 'S' in the TEAMS acronym: Serve Society.

We built a wonderful ecosystem within our society through Mark's membership on the state school board and our involvement with Crestview School. We are building a talent pipeline by investing in children as young as fourth and fifth grade. These children come to Humtown to learn what goes on in a manufacturing business, and then they continue to learn, through practice, in their classrooms.

Mark's mom volunteered at Crestview School to help the children read and learn until she was well into her 90s. She saw it as an opportunity to invest in the learners. As a result, that investment provided much value to her and the children. Her involvement in the school helped Mark recognize the value of establishing a relationship with the local schools.

At around that time, Mark met John Miranda. John had an idea to help children learn differently. He envisioned students learning about careers and practicing project-based learning rather than studying a book and taking tests. In other words, he valued the kind of learning that teaches children how to solve problems in real-life applications.

John needed investors so that he could have teams at schools creating these projects. The students would work under the guidance of a teacher and possibly a workplace manager. The idea was to let the students participate in the project and, in so doing, learn how to solve problems.

Mark presented the students with a problem that Humtown was experiencing that was simple for them to grasp. While working on finding a solution, the children would sometimes be bussed to Humtown; other times, they would spend a week or two in that class learning real-life skills.

CHAPTER 10: FROM DOWNWARD SPIRAL TO UPWARD SYNERGY

One of the problems Mark asked the students to solve involved the sand from the casting mold that stuck to the machine parts. Humtown's production team spent hours every day trying to remove sand from the intricate parts. The students visited the factory to see the problem for themselves and then spent class time working toward a solution.

They learned such skills as teamwork, communicating within a team, brainstorming, evaluating problems and solutions, and other elements of problem-solving. Everything they were taught during that semester was related to Humtown, manufacturing, casting, sand, and molds. For example, math lessons taught them how to calculate volume using sand. They learned the history of foundries and manufacturing. In geography, they learned about sand, erosion, and sustainability.

On presentation day, the school held a project fair where students could showcase their solutions, teaching them skills like public speaking and how to do presentations.

In a different challenge, the students were asked to design something that could be 3D printed. They were given specifications and dimensions to work within. The task incorporated mathematics skills, creative thinking, and design skills. The design that won first place was printed for the team as a reward.

Many manufacturing classes, like Industrial Arts, have been removed from school curriculums, and young people are no longer being trained in manufacturing. In a practical and applicable way, Humtown is investing in society by educating children about the manufacturing industry. Students exposed to this type of project-based learning may decide they want to work at Humtown or other companies in similar industries one day.

The Ohio state governor invited Mark to be a board member on the state board of education. Mark accepted because he wanted to learn what the state was doing to encourage project-based learning in our education system. An integration of a student's academic and vocational interests creates Industrial Athletes that have a passion and purpose. When combining the students vocational and academic interests, greater synergy and energy results, allowing students to perform at a higher level and make the educational experience meaningful.

Mark hopes to help fuel a movement that will not only encourage students to succeed in school, but also find a fulfilling life purpose. In the same way, Humtown's investment in their local school systems has infused education with industrial vision and purpose and has increased their upward spiral of impact.

HUMTOWN'S RESULTS

We created more psychological safety by allowing team members the freedom to FAIL (First Attempt in Learning). This has empowered team members to live fearlessly and take creative risks to learn new things. Mark wakes up daily feeling like it is Christmas because he gets to serve. He *wants* to be at work; he does not just *have* to be there.

The "formula" for Humtown's success is simple: Align company profit goals with the earning goals of Humtown team members. Since the company's Industrial Athletes can influence how much money they make, they have better morale and produce at higher levels while increasing company profits. All stakeholders in the production process at Humtown (company, workers, lending banks, and customers) benefit from that alignment.

While the formula may sound simple, Humtown is a rarity in today's business world. Most companies aim to maximize shareholder value. Humtown's goal is to maximize stakeholder value. The Humtown formula is indeed diametrically opposed to the norm. That is why Mark created a secondary company called DYAMETRIX™ to house the various patents used to transform the workplace into a performance center.

LOCKER ROOM MEETINGS

Humtown has created a shared language through its locker-room meetings, clothing, winners' manual, and training.

Instead of every moment at work being geared toward getting the job done, we take time for *locker-room meetings* to train and develop people.

We do not perceive mistakes as failures but as opportunities to become more brilliant in the business; it is an investment in their education. We offer snacks and have meals available to our team members at no cost. The company removed the vending machines that required cash. The locker-room meetings led to better safety scores and more competent and connected team members.

Companies are responsible for offering training that is not just technical but also helps build good team members. Good training includes resolving conflict, having a difficult conversation, and practicing active listening. These are learnable, teachable skills.

THE MULTIPLIER EFFECT OF VISUAL EARNINGS™

Fantastic financial results were the direct outcome of the "multiplier effect" of **VES**. Company profits are boosted dramatically as workers' earnings increase. The following chart shows how the multiplier effect works:

	Example 1	Example 2	Example 3	Example 4	Real Job Example
% of job rate	70%	100%	150%	200%	1031%
Worker hourly earning rate	$7.00	$10.00	$15.00	$20.00	$103.10
Revenue center "earnings" rate	$140.00	$200.00	$300.00	$400.00	$2,062.00

Note: Revenue center "earnings" rate uses a machine burden rate of $200

Figure 20: The Multiplier Effect

Get to know all stakeholders in your organization and create a high-trust ecosystem that values, invests, nurtures, and replenishes each other by implementing the following ideas.

Stakeholder Map

A stakeholder map is a visual process of identifying prospective stakeholders for your entire organizational ecosystem. Our stakeholder map was built using the acronym (TEAMS): Team Members, Economic Partners, Alliances, the Marketplace, and Society.

Stakeholder Survey

A stakeholder survey is a questionnaire-based quantitative and qualitative tool, most often used to increase your understanding of stakeholders' knowledge, attitudes, perceptions, interests, and experiences.[20] The survey group includes both internal and external stakeholders. We survey all of our team members to get feedback on what is going well and what we can do better.

Analysis

The survey provides quantitative and qualitative data for stakeholder analysis. The analysis examines your employee engagement level and culture and identifies the changes needed for your organization to relate better to relevant and interested stakeholders.

Engagement Strategy

The stakeholder engagement strategy details how your company will keep your stakeholders engaged. It is a way for companies to deliberately engage with people and explicitly document those efforts.

Your Playbook: How You Can Make the Transformation

Upward synergy happens when growth naturally occurs due to the creative cooperation synergy of team members working together for a greater purpose.

To stop the downward spiral and move into upward synergy, consider these points.

1. Understand your stakeholders (fan base, coaches, owners, players, marketing partners, and competitors).

2. Make a deliberate effort to renew a strong and credible brand that goes beyond the four walls of the workplace.

3. Facilitate a shared language, so your team can follow.

4. Become creative in searching outside for new and better ideas and solutions.

Notes
_____
_____
_____
_____
_____
_____

PART 2
CONCLUSION

Culture is the cornerstone of a company and a community. A culture that feels like heaven inspires people to want to be there rather than just having to be there. By seeing people for their true ValYou, the tug-of-war culture can turn into a win-win culture. To do this, make sure that your company's goals are aligned with team members' goals. The people inside can change, and the change can spread to the rest of the community. There are essentially three types of cultures: Win-Lose, Lose-Win, and Win-Win. To determine which culture you have in your company, mark on the continuum where your culture is currently.

- A Win-Lose culture fosters internal competition and is short-term focused. While it can be highly driven and fast-paced, team members may feel like they are losing despite the company's overall progress.
- On the other hand, a Lose-Win culture tends to be overly rigid and conformist, often making leaders feel like they have lost control of the culture.
- The culture we want to focus on is the Win-Win culture. This type of culture emphasizes goal setting, achievement, growth, learning, teamwork, and collaboration.

Figure 21: Win-Win Continuum

PART 3: FROM EMPLOYEE TO INDUSTRIAL ATHLETE

"The earning curve is in the learning curve."

–Brian Cyphert

From
The Industrial Age Egosystem

To
The Industrial Athlete Operating System

Workplace
- ○ Fourth Quarter
- △ Apathy
- □ Chaos

Structural Transformation →

Performance Center
- ○ Winning
- △ Scoreboard Engagement
- □ Clarity

Tug-of-War Culture
- ○ Downward Spiral
- △ Subtle Sabotage
- □ Us vs. Them

Social Transformation →

Win-Win Culture
- ○ Upward Spiral
- △ Trusted Teamwork
- □ Win-Win

Employee
- ○ Unmet Expectations
- △ Disengaged Worker
- □ Surviving

Personal Transformation →

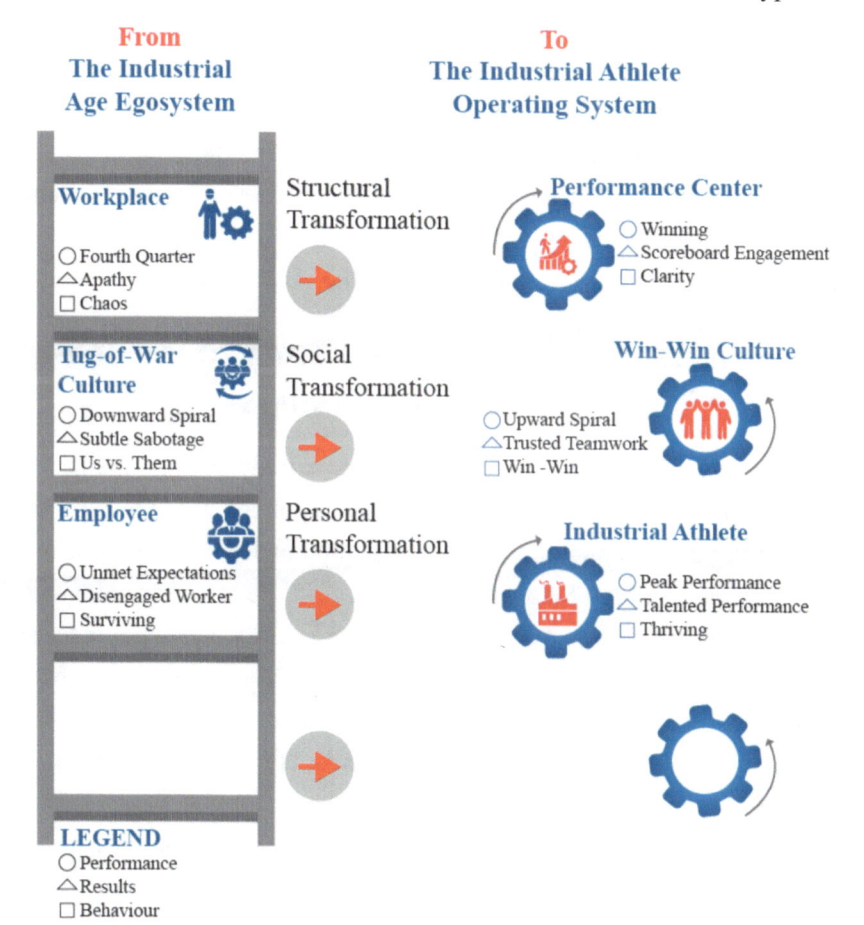

Industrial Athlete
- ○ Peak Performance
- △ Talented Performance
- □ Thriving

LEGEND
- ○ Performance
- △ Results
- □ Behaviour

Figure 22: Employee Transformation Defined

The transformation from employee to Industrial Athlete, is the most personal of an organization's transformations. Employee transformation means galvanizing the individuals to create and sustain organizational transformation at every level. When we unleash the potential of human innovation, we unleash the energy that enables all other parts of the system to succeed.

When functioning as an Industrial Athlete, a person is in the performance zone, engaging their whole being for optimal results. Industrial Athletes use their talents to fill the right positions, are valued for who they are, and perform at the highest levels.

In contrast, an employee may merely mark time for a paycheck, often engaging hands and head, but not heart. It can result in disengagement, high absenteeism, and turnover problems. To tell the difference between an employee and an athlete, let's look at the career of Kurt Warner.

THE TRANSFORMATION OF EMPLOYEE TO ATHLETE: THE TALE OF TWO KURTS

Kurt Warner had one career as an employee and another as a professional athlete. In 1994 Kurt graduated college with the expectation of playing professional football, but that soon ended when the Green Bay Packers released him before the season even started.

Warner needed to pay the bills, so he got a job bagging groceries, stocking shelves, and sweeping floors at a Hy-Vee grocery store back in his hometown in Iowa.[21] He made $5.50 an hour working the night shift so that he could babysit his girlfriend Brenda's two kids while she went to nursing school.

One winter night, Kurt underwent a pivotal experience when he had to pull over to the side of the road.[22]

My car was out of gas, I was a mile from my house, and I didn't have money."

Almost freezing and being helpless and frustrated forced Kurt to acknowledge that he was unhappy working at Hy-Vee because he was not using his talents. He engaged his head and hands but not his heart. He missed playing football so much that while he was supposed to be working, he would take one of the Nerf footballs that were for sale and throw it around to the other employees. Kurt had so many unmet expectations from college that he kept daydreaming about getting out of that job and getting back onto the football field.

Kurt Warner the Athlete

While working at the Hy-Vee grocery store, Kurt put his heart into lifting weights and throwing passes at the University of Northern Iowa's campus. Kurt left his job at Hy-Vee for a chance to show his talent while playing Arena football for three seasons.

In 1998, Kurt's persistence paid off. He landed his first NFL spot with the Rams. He held a backup position until he became a starter for St. Louis after their top quarterback went down with an injury the following season.

Kurt finally reached his goals during his first season as an NFL starting quarterback when he led the Rams to their first-ever title in Super Bowl 34. His offense was coined "The Greatest Show on Turf" because of their record-breaking season. The only player named NFL MVP and Super Bowl MVP, Kurt is also the only undrafted quarterback to lead a team to Super Bowl victory and the first quarterback to win the Super Bowl during his first season.[23]

Kurt married his girlfriend Brenda and started a foundation that has blessed many people. The movie *American Underdog* is the story of his transformation.

Kurt went from employee to professional athlete. It is not out of the range of possibilities to transform from employee to Industrial Athlete.

Kurt Warner found his talent and thrived in his calling as a high-performing professional athlete, in the next three chapters, we will follow the stories of Zach, Carrie, and Brian, three Humtown employees who found their own talents and purpose as Industrial Athletes.

MINDSET, ENGAGEMENT LEVEL, PERFORMANCE RESULTS

The mindset of a disengaged employee is:

"I am my function. I am just here to get a paycheck and to survive."

The engagement level of some employees is:

"I remain disengaged. I am unwilling to give my all and put myself on the line."

The results of an employee might be:

"I am holding back. I do not perform at my highest level or produce winning results."

On the other hand, the mindset of an Industrial Athlete is different:

"I am a part of something bigger than myself. I am here for a purpose. We are all going to win."

The engagement level of an Industrial Athlete is energizing:

"I am all-in to engage my talent."

The results of an Industrial Athlete are fulfilling:

"I am all in, so I perform at my highest level and produce winning results."

	The Industrial Age Egosystem	The Industrial Athlete Operating System
Mindset		
Engagement Level	Treat people like machines	Value people above profits and machines
Performance Results	Bad Profits	Good Profits

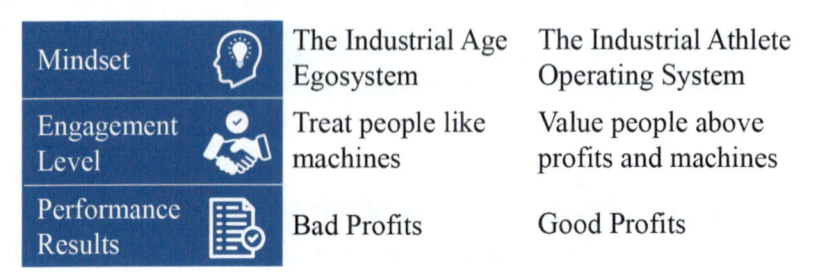

Figure 23: Mindset, Engagement, Performance

An Industrial Athlete achieves personal peak performance by adding maximum value to the team and the customer experience. Team interests are above self-interest, and Industrial Athletes are more concerned with team results than individual results. Trust is felt between team members; the highest level of trust brings a strong emotional connection that can often create a lifetime bond. Industrial Athletes put their whole self in– mind, body, heart, and spirit–for the good of the team. They are fully engaged, and when called upon to perform, they perform at their best.

Some of the differences between an Employee and an Industrial Athlete are listed in Figure 24.

MINDSET	Employee	Industrial Athlete
	Disengaged	Engaged
	Disempowered To Decide	Empowered Decisions
	Work for Employer	Serve All Stakeholders
	Accountable To My Boss	Accountable To All Team Members
	One Dimensional Productivity	Whole Person - Life 360
	What You Do	Who You Are
	Extrinsic only value	Intrinsic Value
	Surviving	Thriving
	Adrift	Positive Intentional Purpose
	Working	Performing

Figure 24: Employee and Industrial Athlete Comparison

CHAPTER 11:
FROM SURVIVING TO THRIVING

"My mission in life is not merely to survive, but to thrive; and to do so with some passion, some compassion, some humor, and some style."

–Maya Angelou

At Humtown, we are aware of the implications of merely surviving. We dreaded making mistakes because they would harm our already meager profits, which were at the bottom end of the range in a highly competitive industry.

Mark explains,

"We were losing in the great game of business before we understood how to help people thrive. We came to the realization that we would be out of business if something did not change as our profit margins continued to erode."

Because we were always in a survival mindset, people were expendable and only as important as the functions they performed. Regardless of our employees' well-being and the problems they brought into the business from home, we had to make a profit every day. Because our staff did not feel valued, they too, were in survival mode, living for five o'clock so they could connect with their family or friends after work.

People were thrown into various functions based on urgent needs. If you had a heartbeat and could get to work, we would put you on a job, even if it was the wrong position for you. Everyone got paid the same–and individual performance was dismal.

These challenges made us realize that the company needed to adopt a different mindset to move from surviving to thriving.

Mark says,

"People were under-performing due to a lack of incentives or burning out because of overwork."

Our production staff often worked eight to twelve hours daily, six or seven days a week.

Mark admits,

"Everyone was always exhausted because our focus was on production alone. We did not realize the value of the person.

We were in survival mode. This burnout bled from leadership to employees and from employees back to leadership, causing frustration, stress, conflict, and inattentiveness to our organizational performance results."

The shift from employee to Industrial Athlete was rooted in recognizing the ValYou in our employees and realizing that we all had to transition from surviving to thriving.

In the following story, we will read how Zach had his well-being restored.

Zach–from surviving to thriving through total well-being.

Once a top Industrial Athlete and coach at Humtown, Zach's world was turned upside down when he found himself in a battle for his life.

Zach loved how the VES allowed him to see his rate continually increase. In fact, he was one of the highest on the Top 10 list. He was a master at fixing the machines and making them outperform the demands of the job. Zach was young, energetic, and healthy and rarely took time off.

Some operators would turn down jobs because they looked unprofitable, but an Industrial Athlete like Zach was able to turn them around and make them highly profitable.

He would do this by calculating what the job entailed and factoring in his highest potential. He had proven to himself what he was capable of, so every time he stepped behind a machine, he would engage his heart as well as his head and hands. Zach was highly creative in increasing his productivity, and his efforts did not go unrewarded. He made $100 per hour on some jobs and turned out as many as 450 parts in an hour on others. Zach turned every job into a winner because it wasn't just about the task; it was about creating greater performance.

He did so well that he was asked to move into a coach position. After he became coach, his shift was so efficient and effective that he was promoted to production coach which would be equivalent to the plant manager.

Unfortunately, Zach started feeling ill, and after a few weeks decided to go to the doctor. He was devastated to learn that he had leukemia. The illness eventually put him completely out of work. Zach was admitted to the hospital. His whole body ached; he couldn't move. He was lying in the hospital bed daily, unsure of what would happen next. He had to go through full-body radiation and chemo before they found a blood donor.

However, just because he wasn't at the plant each day didn't mean he wasn't a part of the Humtown team. Zach's value stretched far beyond his day-to-day abilities. He is a team member, friend, and family member, as well as a co-worker.

Although the treatment worked and Zach is in remission, he is still vulnerable. Zach was excited to come back to Humtown, so he worked with his doctor to return to work slowly. Today Zach is moving from surviving back to thriving in his trade, health, relationships, investments, values, and emotions.

Zach confirmed that an Industrial Athlete must have the drive to perform daily. They must not just come to work for the paycheck. He understands the value of having total well-being as a person to perform at the best of his abilities.

Zach says,

"At Humtown, Mark lets you be your better self. He allows the freedom to have your earnings and self-fulfillment."

HUMTOWN'S DEFINING MOMENT–THE VALYOU OF PEOPLE

In 1990, our accountant said it was time to talk to a bankruptcy attorney to find out our options. It almost appeared that Humtown was no longer surviving, but rather, floundering.

Mark pulled into his driveway on a freezing cold, very dark night in January after meeting with the attorney. He was afraid that he would lose his family home.

But then Mark had a sobering thought.

"I am so concerned about losing my home. What about my employees and their homes if we lose the company? Is their fate secondary to my own?"

Mark returned to Humtown with a question:

"Who is the customer, really?"

When he answered this, he realized that his customers were not just the people buying products, but also the team members building the products. This realization created an ardent desire to treat all vendors, employees, and customers with greater value.

Now, we understand that our employees are more than their job functions. They are human beings at the core. They are someone's valuable and beloved child, partner, or parent with the same challenges, hopes, and needs that we all have. They spend one-third of their lives in the workplace, and we can make a difference in that part of their lives.

Mark explains:

"We had to start from the ground up and intentionally build win-win relationships with our team members who are really our internal customers as we once only did with our external customers.

If we were going to succeed, we had to view everyone not just one-dimensionally, but for their intrinsic human value, and in view of their whole life. We needed to know they had the same needs, desires, and challenges that we all do. On a token level, instead of giving gifts like coffee mugs, hats, shirts, etc., to only our external customers, we started giving these gifts to all team members. We moved from a customer-centric model to an internal customer centric model."

Building on Mark's point, we do not just buy fire extinguishers for the company and train people to save the company if our building catches fire. We also purchase fire extinguishers for each one of them to take to their homes. We do the same with first aid. We buy kits for our people to take home to their families. We recognized each team member's value from a 360-degree point of view: at work, at home, and at play.

Humtown is also one of only two companies that provides food to their staff members for free through the AVI food distribution company.

Mark confirms:

"Our people are our family. If a customer came to Humtown, I would say, 'Let me take you out to eat.'

Some people say, 'Yeah, but a customer doesn't come in every day.'

Then I say, 'Yes, they do.'

My customers come here every day; they are my team members, so I 'take them out to eat' each day."

THRIVING WITH TOTAL WELL-BEING

Total well-being is our quality of life. People define this in terms of life satisfaction, a sense of meaning or purpose, good mental health, and the ability to be resilient to stress. It is what a person finds to be intrinsically valuable and good in their life.

Basketball teams that have identified talent as the chief ingredient in recruiting will look for someone who is most fit for the position. Balanced well-being in all areas of life will provide the clear-minded focus needed to perform best during the game.

Industrial Athletes also tend to perform at a higher level when they have well-being in all areas of life. Personal problems are often brought to work, so it is beneficial for an organization to value its team members' whole lives.

We designed THRIVE 360 acronym as a life wheel for organizations, coaches, and Industrial Athletes to use in helping all team members become satisfied and fulfilled. The THRIVE 360 acronym is a tool and program that allows people to create a life vision and evaluate their current state and plan with the help of coaching.

The word *thrive* means *"prospering, flourishing, or developing well."* The THRIVE 360 acronym addresses these spheres:

- **T**rade: the focus of our career.
- **H**ealth: our fitness, nutrition, and quantity of energy.
- **R**elationships: our engagement with the people around us.
- **I**nvestment: our relationship with money.
- **V**alues: the force of our spiritual energy.
- **E**motions: the emotional quality of our life.

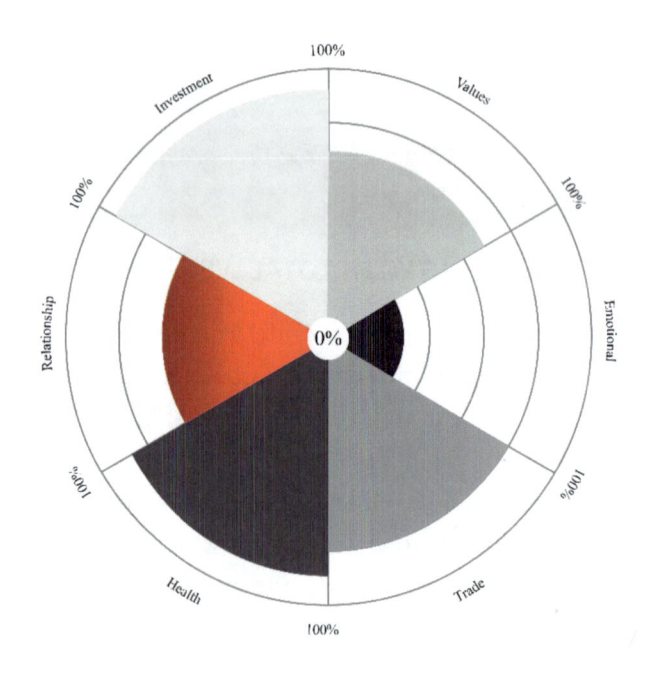

Figure 25: THRIVE 360

Figure 25 illustrates an example of the spheres in a sample person's life, and how committed they are to each of them. If this were a real person, they would have an imbalance and would not be thriving in the areas of relationships, values, and emotions. And where this is an imbalance, there isn't THRIVE 360 well-being.

Thriving: Rooted in ValYou

The first part of the transition from employee to Industrial Athlete is the shift from surviving to thriving. When we discovered the ValYou in our people, we could appreciate them from a 360-degree point of view. We could appreciate Zach through the ups and downs of his health battles and make sure he remained a part of the team because he is not just an employee but a family member. Suppose all Industrial Athletes can learn the value of taking care of themselves from a 360-degree perspective. In that case, we will have one healthy team.

Your Playbook: How You Can Make the Transformation

Because humans are complex energy systems, we need to thrive and have well-being in every area of our lives. Team members can THRIVE if they know that they can talk to someone about the stresses in their lives.

Keys to success include providing a human resources specialist, life coach, or manager, with the skills to coach people through their life challenges.

Move from surviving to thriving by considering these points.

1. Do you use a model to help people develop well-being in their whole lives?

2. Do you ever see people bringing their stresses from home into the workplace?

3. How do you see that impacting their quality of work?

4. Ask your other leaders if they experience outside pressures impacting inside performance.

Notes:
_____
_____
_____
_____
_____
_____

CHAPTER 12:
FROM DISENGAGED WORKER
TO TALENTED TEAM MEMBER

"Do you want to make a living, or do you want to make a difference? Therein lies the difference between work and performing in a career that you love."

–Mark Lamoncha

The next dimension in the transformation from employee to Industrial Athlete is talent. The key to unlocking high performance is finding the right fit between a person's talents and their position.

A DEFINING MOMENT FOR TALENT

Discovering and developing talent is the greatest factor in building a winning organization. National championship basketball coach John Wooden said,

"No matter your total success in the coaching profession, it all comes down to a single factor: TALENT!" [24]

Suppose you coach a basketball team. In basketball, recruiting is the team's lifeblood because talent is primary. When recruiting, you think that a taller, quicker, and stronger player is talented. When leading an organization, discovering, recruiting, and developing talent is vital to building high-performing teams. We have found that being intentional about matching people with their talent and the right position has been a difference maker for cultivating a high-performance Industrial Athlete culture.

Carrie–from disengaged worker to talented industrial athlete

Because of a toxic work environment and lack of talent match at her previous job, Carrie struggled to find a fit. Gallup's comprehensive 2015 study uncovered a harsh truth: 75 percent of people quit their jobs to "get away from their manager" at some point in their career. This was certainly true for Carrie. Due to recurrent negativity, misplacement, and lack of team spirit in the work environment, she hated her former job so much that she became known as a misfit absentee and was almost fired.

After Carrie got laid off work when her former company left the area, she stayed at home for as long as her unemployment insurance would allow. She was not motivated to work because of her previous experience. When it came time for her to work again, she took a job at Humtown, expecting more of the same. Carrie was pleasantly surprised to find a very different situation to the one she had escaped from.

When she came to Humtown, she was able to work in a job that matched her talent, skills, and interests. Now, Carrie's job satisfaction comes not just from her paycheck but also from a sense of belonging, finding the right fit, and an environment that incentivizes applied learning and growth.

THE RIGHT FIT FOR THE RIGHT JOB

Humtown had a big machine that ran all the time, and it took a team of six people to work it. Before, each person was just assigned a spot, regardless of their strengths. Now, the coaches take note of people's talents and performance and match individuals with the most suitable position.

Mark has often said,

> *"The greatest energy on earth is human potential. Instead of just haphazardly educating people, we need to find out what people are meant to be and focus our education on their interests. Interest fuels passion. Passion fuels focus, intensity, and performance."*

CHAPTER 12: FROM DISENGAGED WORKER TO TALENTED TEAM MEMBER

Figure 26. shows the progression of interest fueling purpose, which in turn fuels passion, and engagement.

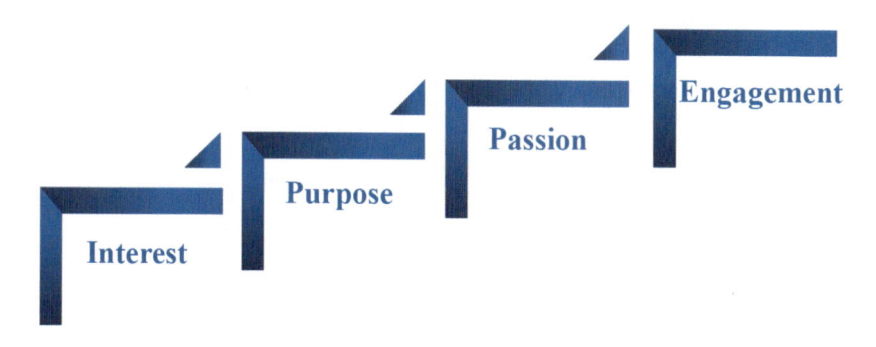

Figure 26: Interest, Purpose, Passion, Engagement

Although Mark grew up in the family business and knew the manufacturing processes extremely well, he and his staff had no education or training in talent management. Knowing that we needed a change at Humtown, we did a talent audit with consultant Joe Davenport. Joe was introduced to Humtown more than 20 years ago when the company had not made a profit for 36 consecutive months.

Joe recommended that Humtown conduct a talent audit of the company's workforce using a job-matching assessment to determine whether the company had the right people performing the right activities. The audit showed that analyzing people's interests, thinking styles, and behavioral traits and matching them with our job position benchmark helped them perform better, as shown in Figure 27.

Person	Position
■ Thinking Style	■ Thinking Style
■ Behavior	■ Behavior
■ Interest	■ Interest

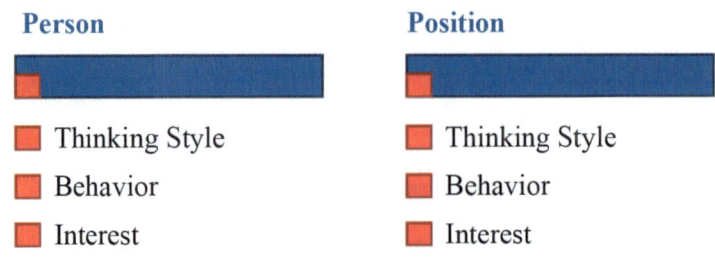

Figure 27: Talent Match

Talent matching enhances productivity, quality, safety, and customer service. When people use their unique talents, their engagement levels increase significantly.

Mark clarifies,

"Aligning talent to the position can be compared to two different pilots in the military. The thinking style, interest, and behavior of a C130 pilot would be far different from that of a fighter jet pilot. A C130 pilot is not going to have the natural reaction time that a fighter jet pilot will have. And a fighter jet pilot will be bored to death in the C130. If a fighter pilot is flying a C130 they are not vertically aligned around their thinking style, interest, and behavior."

Joe came in to help reverse engineer the talent, interest level, behavior traits, and thinking style of a position, not the person. Most tests only test the person but not in relation or parity to the position. If team members are shifted to match positions, there is greater synergy and productivity.

We now strive to use "tools" to enhance the engagement of our employees. First, we know workers with personal attributes matching their jobs will be more engaged. We use a talent matching assessment for all employees, from janitors to leaders. The assessment matches candidates with positions where they will perform well and enjoy their work. It also identifies ways to enhance performance and maximize an individual's contribution to an organization.[25]

Sheri Lamoncha explains:

CHAPTER 12: FROM DISENGAGED WORKER TO TALENTED TEAM MEMBER

"It was a huge change for us to understand and match a person's talent with the job. It provided confidence that this was the best person suited for this position."

Factory workers are specifically screened for attributes that make them a great match for the VES technology and the high-performing culture at Humtown. Industrial Athletes need the appropriate thinking style, behavioral traits, and motivational interests to perform at a high level, day-in and day-out. They also need to be self-motivated and want to make as much money as possible within the system.

Joe tells of a time when talent and job matching resulted in a win-win for Humtown and a talented machine operator:

"I still remember the first time we used the talent and job matching tool effectively at Humtown. We had a job opening for a coach on another shift. The other coach was moving away, and Mark came to me and said,

"We need to hire somebody. Run an ad quickly."

And I said, "Wait, what? Whoa, whoa, whoa. Maybe there is somebody here we could put in that position."

Mark said, "What do you mean?"

So, I showed him the talent database, and we saw a person whose talent would be a good match for the job. The person was on the second shift, but they didn't have any coaching background.

So, I said, "I will train them over the next few months, and then you will then have a coach for that position."

Mark said, "Okay. The only problem is that person quit this morning."

I asked, "Why did they quit?"

Mark said, "They weren't earning enough yet."

I asked how much money they were making and how much money they needed to earn. The coaching position would provide enough money for them to stay. I told Mark, "We can solve two problems at once. They will get the money they need, and you will get the coach you need."

So, I trained them and within a couple of months they were the top-performing coach. The shift became the highest performing shift in the company."

Finding a worker's best fit resulted in success for the coach, success for the employees, success for the shift, and success for the company.

The figures below illustrate the difference between an employees' thinking style, behavioral traits, and interests before (Figure 28) and after (Figure 29) a job matching exercise.

Overall Job Match	48%
Thinking Style	25%
Behavioral Traits	63%
Interests	65%

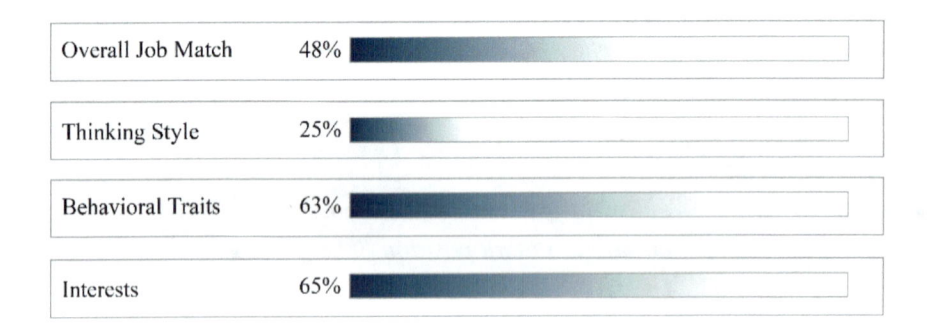

Figure 28: Before Talent Example 48%

Overall Job Match	86%
Thinking Style	81%
Behavioral Traits	86%
Interests	94%

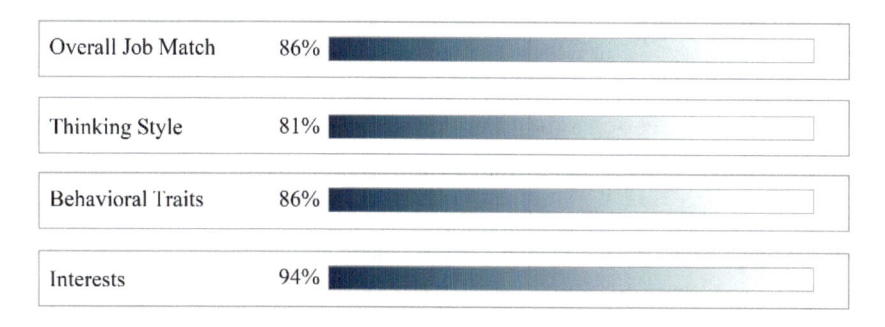

Figure 29: After Talent Example 86%

We made a profit three months after reviewing the talent audit results and implementing the necessary changes. This resulted in greater job satisfaction and increased personal responsibility for the work.

Before, the talent audit and VES, mistakes resulted in eight percent scrap; since, scrap has dropped by more than five percent. That audit process was transformative for the business and laid the groundwork for talent management to become a key component of our operations.

Character + Talent + Performance = Results

A disengaged employee is unproductive and does not consider the organization's best interests. They are thinking about themselves, their wants, their needs, and how dissatisfied they are. Once a person's skills and talents are matched to their job, they shift from just doing an assigned task to performing at their peak.

Your Playbook: How You Can Make the Transformation

As we face ever-changing demands in our work world, commitment to know and grow our unique talent and skill through experience, knowledge, and practice is essential. In sports, talent is easily identified—who is bigger, stronger, and faster? In business, what are the criteria to use?

Consider these points in transforming disengaged workers into talented team members.

1. How do you define unique talent in your industry?

2. Is everyone in the right job for their skill set?

3. Do you see people discovering and developing their talent to continually improve organizational performance?

4. Are you providing a talent discovery and development process?

Notes

_____
_____
_____
_____
_____

CHAPTER 13:
FROM UNMET EXPECTATIONS TO PEAK PERFORMANCE

"Don't lower your expectations to meet your performance. Raise your level of performance to meet your expectations. Expect the best of yourself, and then do what is necessary to make it a reality."

–Ralph Marston

A peak performer maximizes output and achieves the best possible results.

In basketball, a peak performer could score many points, be good at defense, steal the ball, block shots, rebound well, and contribute to a winning team.

In business, high performance is evaluated on production, sales, customer service, and on-time delivery in the workplace.

At Humtown, our peak performance goals are:

Make it safe.

Make it right.

Make it above rate.

Gallup breaks down the definition of performance:

"Any outcome that is deemed valuable by either an external or internal customer"[26]

A player in the peak performance state is identified as being "in the zone."

Basketball players report that the hoop looks bigger in the zone, and golfers get in a rhythm and make all their putts.

When the late Kobe Bryant scored 81 points in one game, he said he was in the zone and could hardly miss the hoop. Tiger Woods got into the zone so much in his first decade of professional golf that people nicknamed his optimal performance the "Tiger Zone."

Brian's transformation: from unmet expectations to peak performer

Brian is one of the first team members to identify as an Industrial Athlete because he found his talent in a place that allowed him to experiment and improve. Brian no longer lived with unmet expectations, rather, he became a peak performer. He continued to learn until he performed at a level that took him to #1 on the top 10 Humtown performance scoreboard repeatedly.

When Brian was young, he dropped out of high school and hopped from job to job, searching for success. After he lost his job at a previous employer, he couldn't find another because he had a very specific skill set. He landed at Humtown during the financial slump of 2008 when the job market was tight, but he had no intention of staying for the long term.

Despite an initial shaky start, Brian more than doubled his earnings within his first five years, specifically after the implementation of the VES. Before technology was fully integrated into the Visual Earnings™ System, Brian manually tracked and journaled what was repeatable by customer and job, and logged his own rates for each job as he worked. He kept track of the problems and what it took to resolve them, so that he would know what to do if it happened again. This was how Brian would enter into the zone. He was so astute that he learned how many seconds were in a 6-hour shift to work on shortening his machine run times so that he could be more productive.

Working at Humtown positively impacted Brian. Not just because of the incentives, but because of the genuine opportunities to learn and grow, and because of Mark's leadership style, which inspired Brian greatly.

At one point, Brian was offered his old job back where he had made good money at a fixed rate. But after careful consideration, Brian decided

CHAPTER 13: FROM UNMET EXPECTATIONS TO PEAK PERFORMANCE

to stay at Humtown because he realized that the more he learned, the more he earned.

He had previously worked in companies with incentive programs, but the bar was often unrealistically high, or arbitrarily raised once anyone reached it. In his early days at Humtown, he often wondered when they would change the rates to unfairly manipulate his earnings. But Mark never did. On the contrary, he promoted increased earning through learning, creating a win-win.

Brian explains:

"You're trying to outdo yourself. If you are competitive, you want to be the person on the floor with the highest rate. Competing with someone else can be fun. But ultimately, you're competing for your own personal record."

Being a fierce competitor, Brian knew it was only a matter of time before he achieved his goal of being named one of the top ten machine operators on the floor.

Figure 30 is an example of Humtown's top 10 scoreboard.

NAME	DATE	JOB NUM	QTY	EFF%	SCRAP%
Jane Doe	4/28/2020	024378	109	483%	7%
Jane Doe	9/12/2019	013929	171	418%	0%
Richard Roe	12/29/2014	014656	221	371%	0%
Joe Citizen	5/19/2018	015726	262	344%	344%
Jane Citizen	11/9/2017	014428	213	304%	2%
Average Joe	2/19/2018	015154	112	232%	0%
JaneJ. Doe	11/9/2017	014366	332	229%	4%
Renee Roe	11/30/2016	011674	73	217%	3%
John J. Citizen	8/4/2015	013584	356	185%	7%
John J. Citizen	8/26/2012	013773	436	178%	0%

Figure 30: Top 10 List

IN THE PEAK PERFORMANCE ZONE

A study by McKinsey & Company tracked top executives for ten years. They concluded that they were five times more productive in the mental state known as "the zone."

An Industrial Athlete is in the zone when fully immersed in a feeling of energized focus, full involvement, and enjoyment in the activity.[27]

The Yerkes-Dodson Law provides a visual for reaching an optimal level of performance, as illustrated in Figure 31. It states that performance increases with physiological or mental arousal, but only up to a point. When levels of arousal are too high, performance decreases.[28] A peak performer must remain between complacency and burnout.

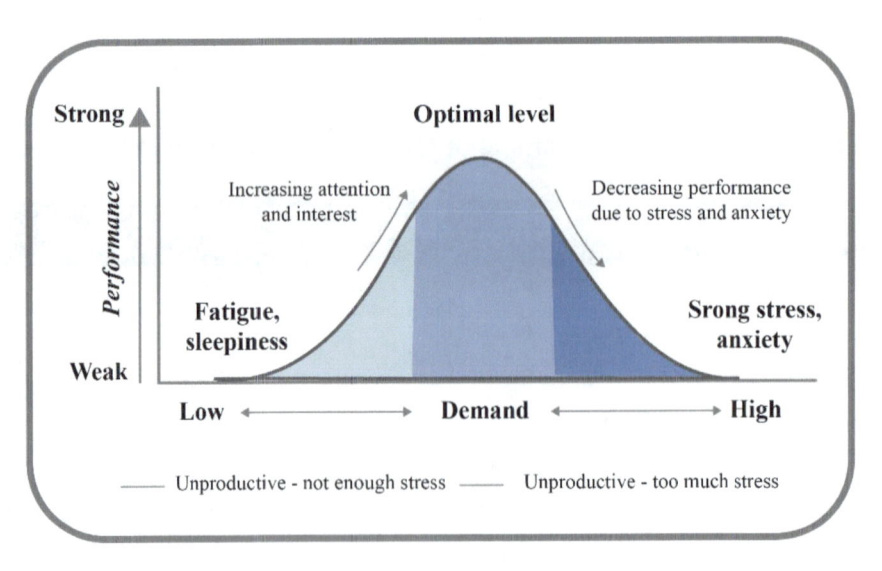

Figure 31: Yerkes-Dodson Performance Curve

We moved to six-hour shifts. It helps keep our Industrial Athletes from burnout, allowing them to work in the zone for shorter bursts. After work hours, they can enjoy a balanced lifestyle and return for their next shift

CHAPTER 13: FROM UNMET EXPECTATIONS TO PEAK PERFORMANCE

renewed. This is the embodiment of THRIVE 360 and allows our Industrial Athletes to hit the peak performance state again and again.

Mihaly Csikszentmihalyi put the science to the zone when he interviewed artists, athletes, and musicians to better understand these intrinsically motivating experiences. He discovered an elevated level of engagement, which he termed "flow."

When in the state of flow, or the zone, we lose our sense of self, forgetting about our worries and concerns. The experience is intrinsically rewarding and our performance soars. Operating in the zone takes the full attention and engagement of our body, mind, soul, and spirit—all four dimensions of our being. Everything just clicks, and we feel like we can do no wrong. We achieve personal bests, yet our performance feels effortless.[29]

To allow us to flow in the zone, our work must offer us these nine elements:

- Be challenging within our abilities.
- Offer clear goals where we know what we need to do.
- Offer immediate feedback.
- Provide complete focus on the action.
- Offer a lack of distractions or mind-wandering.
- Provide an absence of fear of failure.
- Nurture a lack of self-consciousness.
- Provide a loss of awareness of time passing.
- Result in overall fulfillment or enjoyment.

The resounding ripple effect of being in this optimal performance state contributes to greater employee job performance, productivity, teamwork, company profits, and fulfillment for themselves and others. Instead of companies losing 85 percent of their productivity, they collectively achieve more from everyone.

In our case, we learned that the Visual Earnings™ System helps our team members perform at their peak because of real-time engagement, feedback, and rewards. The feedback immediately shows them what they are earning at that moment, which has significantly increased their productivity.

Optimal engagement is found in the zone

By shifting from employees stagnating in unmet expectation to Industrial Athletes capable of operating in the zone, our team members increased their performance results and paychecks from between 150 to 400 percent.

By 2012, 26 people were producing the same product sales as the company did with a much larger workforce in 2008. Unlocking the human potential of Humtown's team members was the key to redefining our competitive advantage.

In addition, research into the best practices for increasing productivity led us to study employee engagement. We empower our employees in several ways, but engagement is the cornerstone.

The results of the implementation of the VES and the corresponding changes in Humtown's talent and culture were staggering. Productivity soared by more than 400 percent, and staff turnover plummeted from 70 percent to less than five. The job matching assessment we addressed earlier in the book has been instrumental in boosting employee engagement and earnings while providing a sense of self-fulfillment to the workers. Making sure that the right people were at the "controls" of the VES continues to change the culture at Humtown in an incredibly positive way.

CHAPTER 13: FROM UNMET EXPECTATIONS TO PEAK PERFORMANCE

Your Playbook: How You Can Make the Transformation

To generate optimal lasting results at an individual level, each person must balance the demand for performance with the appropriate measure of stress and recurrent rest and renewal. Are you helping your team members develop the appropriate capacity to perform in the face of everyday work demands?

Work through these questions to bring about the transformation that leads to peak performance.

1. Do you use Life Wheel Goals, Stress/Performance Evaluator?

2. Do you feel your team members are reaching their peak potential?

3. Do you ever feel that they are not performing to the best of their abilities?

4. Do they have the support and clarity they need to achieve their best for themselves and the team?

Notes:
_____
_____
_____
_____
_____
_____

PART 3
CONCLUSION

Because of Mark's vision for what Humtown could achieve and a belief in the power of his people to get the job done, the business now enjoys record production levels. The higher employee pay rates, more competitive pricing on parts, lower labor and healthcare costs, and low staff turnover prove that the talent management initiatives are a meaningful success.[30]

The trust-performance matrix is tool that the Navy Seals use and is a way that you can quickly think about your industrial athletes. You have to know how to measure performance and high trust. In this matrix, circle where your team members are to assess the level of trust and performance.

High Performance Low Trust	High Performance High Trust
Low Performance Low Trust	Low Performance High Trust

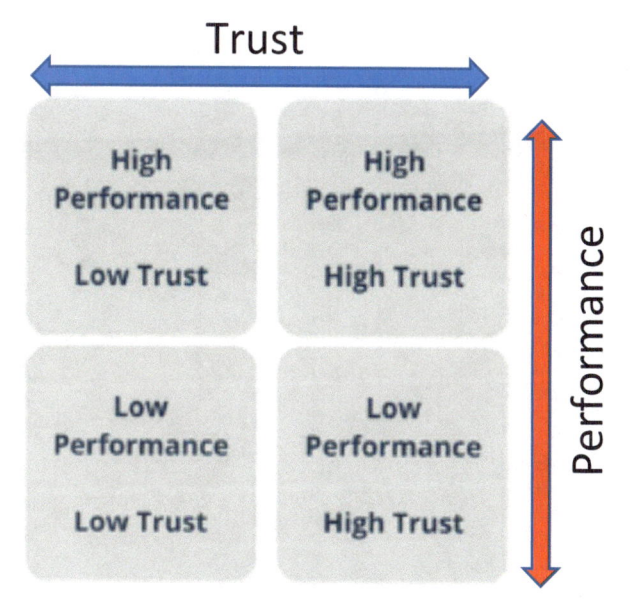

Figure 32: Trust/Performance Matrix

PART 4: FROM BOSS TO COACH

"Leadership is the highest of the arts, simply because it enables all the other arts and professions to work."

–Stephen R. Covey.

From
The Industrial Age Egosystem

To
The Industrial Athlete Operating System

Workplace
- ○ Fourth Quarter
- △ Apathy
- □ Chaos

Structural Transformation →

Performance Center
- ○ Winning
- △ Scoreboard Engagement
- □ Clarity

Tug-of-War Culture
- ○ Downward Spiral
- △ Subtle Sabotage
- □ Us vs. Them

Social Transformation →

Win-Win Culture
- ○ Upward Spiral
- △ Trusted Teamwork
- □ Win-Win

Employee
- ○ Unmet Expectations
- △ Disengaged Worker
- □ Surviving

Personal Transformation →

Industrial Athlete
- ○ Peak Performance
- △ Talented Performance
- □ Thriving

Boss
- ○ Micro-Managed
- △ Task Master
- □ Command and Control

Management Transformation →

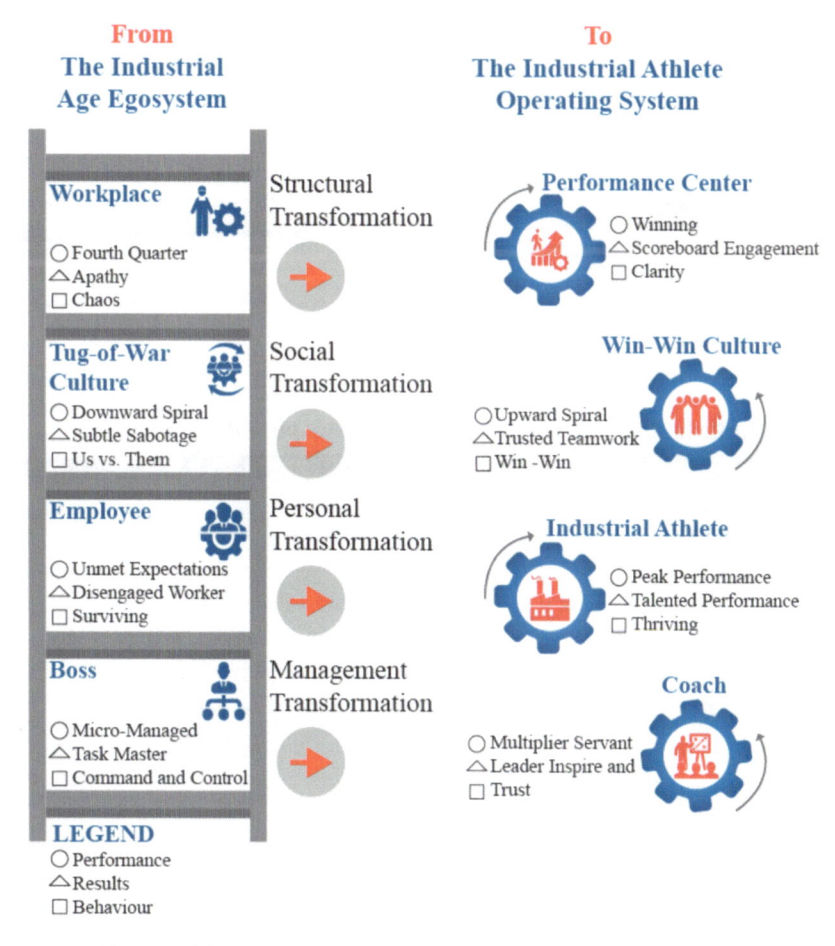

Coach
- ○ Multiplier Servant
- △ Leader Inspire and
- □ Trust

LEGEND
- ○ Performance
- △ Results
- □ Behaviour

Figure 33: Management Transformation Defined

In Part 4, we discuss the fourth transformation, which enables managers to think like coaches rather than bosses. Bosses typically leave employees feeling demotivated at best and rebellious at worst. In contrast, coaches perceive peoples' talents, identify with them, and encourage teams to work together for a greater shared purpose.

Consequently, the boss-to-coach transformation enables managers to think and act like coaches, and achieve high-performance coaching results rather than the outdated resistance that an industrial-age supervisor receives from employees.

The boss mindset often comes across as commanding and controlling, trying to shape others into their projected image. As a result, team members are often disengaged, unmotivated, and just working to collect a paycheck and go home.

In contrast, coaching perceives a person's needs, identifies with them, and actively supports their real self to work together on a team for a greater shared purpose. This results in people being "all in" with their whole hearts to help the organization win.

THE SCRAP OF SAND AND THE EAGLE

Mark shares a time when a team member provided him with one of his favorite analogies about the difference between a boss and a coach.

"We make our cores out of sand; therefore, we often have leftovers. One day, Tom came into my office and asked me if he could take some leftover scrap sand.

I said, "Of course!" because the scrap was headed for a landfill, never to be seen again. When I came in on Monday morning, Tom handed me an eagle that he beautifully crafted from the scrap sand."

The realistic appearance of the eagle made it hard to believe the creature was made of discarded sand.

Much like Michelangelo when he sculpted David from the chunk of granite, Tom saw a magnificent eagle within the sand before his tools started to form it. He skillfully worked to remove the leftover sand that held the eagle captive.

Figure 34: The Scrap and the Eagle

Which do you want for your team: the leftovers of their talent or an eagle?

Relationships are paramount because bossing people by merely citing rules, regulations, and policies tends to diminish their abilities. Instead, a coach, encourages team members to release their own creative ability.

Coaching helps team members rise above challenges to own their problems and engage their heads, hands, and hearts. Your actions as a coach should inspire, serve, and multiply to bring forth eagles.

Mark continues,

"What we threw out, Tom saw potential in. We saw pieces of scrap sand; he saw an eagle. Recognizing the potential in others is what great coaches do."

THE CONTRAST BETWEEN BOSS AND COACH

A great coach can unearth talent in the same way that someone takes a diamond in the rough and polishes it. Every facet of the brilliance and brightness of that talent shines in everything they do.

When there is a change from boss to coach, the tone or atmosphere in the workplace changes. In other words, even though their roles and responsibilities are the same, the outcome of their behavior on those they supervise is significantly different. Unlike a traditional supervisor who yells and blames employees for not knowing what to do, a coach inspires team members to reach their full capability.

Bosses dictate what needs to be done in many businesses, even though they are less informed than the team members closest to the action.

Think about it. We don't see coaches playing in a sports competition. When the whistle blows and the game begins, the coaches do not run onto the field, the ice, or the court; the players do. In a business sense, the "players" are serving customers or making the product, but in many companies, their opinions do not count. This could be one of the biggest reasons why Gallup found that the manager determines 70 percent of the variance in team engagement. When people are treated like machines, they will act like machines and not think for themselves.

Managers and supervisors can better engage team members and help them perform optimally in their jobs when they transform to a coach approach. The following table highlights some other differentiators:

Boss	Coach
Suspicious	Trust
Control and Contain	Release Potential
Command and Control	Inspire
Makes All Decisions	Helps Others and Makes Decisions
Gives Orders	Listens and Collaborates
Dictates Methods	Establishes Boundaries
Lead by Position	Leads with Influence
Transactional	Transformational

Figure 35: Boss vs Coach Approach

The **Industrial Athlete Operating System** empowers team members to reach their highest capacity by shifting from a bossing management style–which often leads to mistrust and disempowerment–to focusing on the core elements of great coaching to mentor, inspire, practice servant leadership, and multiply the efforts of all team members.

CHAPTER 14:

FROM COMMAND AND CONTROL TO INSPIRE AND TRUST

"People don't care how much you know until they know how much you care."

–Theodore Roosevelt

To better understand the transformation from boss to coach, imagine that you are the head basketball coach for a small-town community hoping to contend for a state championship. What would you need to do to successfully develop your team?

To begin, you must inspire your players and give them hope for the coming season. As a coach, you must clearly define where the team is going. Are we looking to make the playoffs this year? Can we win the conference title? What do we need to do to contend for the state championship?

Without hungry and willing team members, it will be hard for you to lead your team to success.

A coach who inspires from within engages team members by connecting their intrinsic motivation with the team's collective goals to create a shared vision. Once this is done, the team will commit their heads, hands, and hearts to work together to achieve success.

To generate a commitment from team members, a coach needs to know each person's intrinsic motivation, clarify the team's goals, then successfully tie them together.

HUMTOWN'S OLD-SCHOOL MANAGEMENT STYLE

For three decades our unsuccessful former management style was influenced by the early Industrial Age. This command-and-control style said, "Show up, and we will tell you what to do." Unfortunately, we were disempowering our people by treating them like machines and constricting their capability without knowing it. As a result, we constantly had high employee turnover.

Brian says that, back then, if anyone had a problem and they needed help, the response from Humtown management was dismissive.

"Figure it out," or
"What are you asking me for?" or
"It's your problem, not mine."

Before the feedback and visual scoreboard of the VES there was no incentive for anyone to work any harder. The supervisors had to boss and push people and tell them what to do.

"Keep going, guys. We need to get to the rate. We need to do this. We need more done."

Our supervisors had to make sure everyone stayed at their machines. They kept prodding them like cattle to get more work from them because they were not being incentivized. As a result, the employees paid little regard to how fast or slow they worked. They would take long smoke breaks or bathroom breaks. There was no urgency to get back to production. When the boss was away, they would stop work and chat. The burden of responsibility was on the supervisor to keep everybody going.

Organizations rely on managers to motivate team members. However, a study by CareerBuilder.com found that 58 percent of managers said they did not receive any management training.

The pervasive boss mindset of the Industrial Age that still dominates today's workplace will not work in Industry 4.0. Living in the Fourth Industrial age but leading with an earlier industrial management style creates subtle sabotage and employee disengagement.

We still see the residual effect of the tug-of-war between management and employees from the first three Industrial Ages. The emerging generation does not respond well to old-school command-and-control supervision.

These new team members want coaches who inspire them, communicate clearly, and help them develop their purpose and talents. They want a balance of expectations to motivate them to use their skills to the fullest but not to a level that will cause anxiety.

Any boss, supervisor, or manager who wants to be a coach must change from the old way of thinking that said:

"I will command and control you without taking time to find out what your true skills are."

Shifting to a coach approach that actively listens to their team members to understand their intrinsic needs provides a healthy culture.

A manager who leads high-performing teams must have the right mindset and skillset. The manager's most important objective is to fully engage their team members' heads, hearts, hands, and whole being, like a coach. Once this is achieved, coaches can create trust, vision, collaboration, and accountability within teams.

A DEFINING MOMENT TO MOVE TO COACHING

A real coach—one who coaches an athlete to win and become a winner—takes the time and interest to invest in the athletes from the inside out. The coach's mission is to understand them, their life, and their interests, and work together to find their true undeveloped talents to become the best version of themselves.

Mark explains:

"When Sheri and I were traveling back and forth to the hockey games, I realized they were not bosses teaching my children hockey; they were coaches. At once, I realized the difference between coaching winners and coaching just to win a game at any cost. It is the kids who need to have the desire to succeed. Coaches who want it more than the kids often push too hard, creating resistance from the student-athletes."

Taking advantage of people's skills and abilities for maximum profitability tends to lock up their capability. A coach who coaches to win games for selfish reasons at the expense of (or despite) the athlete's true talents, is no better than a boss, supervisor, or manager who controls the worker's output for their personal or the company's corporate gain.

Although the Visual Earnings™ System was more of a technological concept, it stimulated better productivity, boosted employee learning, and resulted in a change in managerial thinking. Coaching surpassed the command-and-control structure in fast-tracking employees' learning curves, turning them into high-performing Industrial Athletes.

THE IMPACT OF A PERFORMANCE CENTER ON BOSS VS. COACH

When we initiated the Visual Earnings™ System, this shifted the responsibility from the supervisor to the team members. Seeing their earnings in real-time and knowing their efforts would be rewarded was all the motivation the Industrial Athletes needed to move their performance numbers by producing more. They no longer needed a supervisor prodding them.

With the Visual Earnings™ System, the team members and operators on the floor eventually became so enthusiastic about increasing their earning rate and moving the numbers on the scoreboard that they no longer wanted to waste time.

While they were being productive, their earning rate was going up. For example, if Carrie is not productive, she will make a $10-an-hour base rate, and, at the end of the week, she will walk home with $400. On the other hand, if Carrie is productive, she can walk home with $1,500. Imagine being hired at $400 a week and turning it into $1,500! That is exactly what Carrie did before she became a coach. The VES became a motivating force for team members. Supervision was no longer needed, so the shift to coaching was pertinent. Mark describes the results:

"By incentivizing people with the Visual Earnings™ System, our Industrial Athletes can see their earnings in real-time. With a

real-time feedback gamification tool, they could immediately see their personal earnings and production rate. VES provides empowerment to self-management keeping the Industrial Athlete in a state of peak performance.

The earning rate helped us with the transition from supervising to coaching. This also helped us make our decision to provide free food in the locker room. Our team members would go in when they needed to eat, but they would return to their machines without delay because they did not want to lose production time. Every moment they are not working causes their earning rate to drop."

If the burden of responsibility is on the manager to get things done, then they are responsible for making the change. However, when the employee shifts to an Industrial Athlete with a visual incentive to continually improve, they become more responsible. They no longer need a boss pushing them, rather, they need a coach supporting them. Coaches are not managing; they are inspiring and trusting. They walk alongside the team instead of cracking a whip and trying to make them do what they want them to do.

With self-management comes accountability. The instant feedback causes the Industrial Athlete to see how their behavior affects their earnings.

COACHING TAPS INTO INTRINSIC MOTIVATION

Coaching taps into intrinsic motivation, where a boss is typically still using extrinsic motivation. Intrinsic motivation refers to the drive to engage in an activity for its own sake, for the enjoyment, satisfaction, or challenge that it provides. This type of motivation comes from within, rather than from external factors such as rewards or punishments.

Extrinsic motivation, on the other hand, refers to the drive to engage in an activity due to external rewards or consequences. For example, doing a task to receive a monetary reward or to avoid punishment.

Both forms of motivation can coexist and influence behavior, but intrinsic motivation tends to lead to better outcomes, such as increased creativity, persistence, and engagement in the task.

CHAPTER 14: FROM COMMAND AND CONTROL TO INSPIRE AND TRUST

Your Playbook: How You Can Make the Transformation

A newer approach to coaching that inspires and trusts rather than commands and controls is predicated on the idea that individuals are inherently creative, capable of working together, and brimming with untapped possibilities. People that work under this kind of coach are motivated to improve themselves and their job to become the finest versions of themselves.

To create valuable outcomes for our stakeholders, we need coaches to be both high performing and trustworthy. Coaches intrinsically inspire their team members to develop the talent that grows them into their full ability.

Consider these points to move from a place of command and control to one of inspire and trust.

1. Provide coaches with a high trust/high-performance matrix to measure their ability to inspire and trust.

2. What realistic goal can we set to create buy-in?

3. How can we help team members clarify their personal and team goals and action plans?

Notes
_____
_____
_____
_____
_____

CHAPTER 15:
FROM TASKMASTER TO SERVANT LEADER

"We make a living by what we get. We make a life by what we give."

–James Kouzes

Imagine again that you are coaching your small-town basketball team. They understand the expectations, and they believe that they can have a great season. As a coach, you must now create the conditions where that vision becomes a reality. Your role is ultimately empowering your team members to play at their peak. You must communicate with enough psychological safety that their brains will function at their full capacity.

In addition to inspiring from within, a coach acts as a servant leader to their team members. With the Industrial Athlete taking the initiative and being as productive as possible, the coach can assist the team members in finding out if they need anything to maximize their performance. In other words, the coach serves the team member's desire to succeed.

HOW MARK LEARNED TO SERVE

Mark, who is a second-generation family business owner, shares from his personal experience a situation that unfolded between himself and his father. He then shares a transition moment where he learned the value of servant leadership from Benny Gonzales, a service station owner.

Mark tells this story:

"I started working at Humtown from age 12 until 17, but I never felt connected to pattern making. I later discovered I lacked spatial perception and could not see things three-dimensionally. I could not become passionate about this work because the spatial perception deficit prevented me from seeing the part depicted in the drawings.

This led to frustration for my father and me. It caused consternation because my dad envisioned me to be a pattern maker. But because I could not see things the way he saw them, I could not follow in his business.

I left and went to work at a service station. There I learned more from Benny Gonzales about serving others than I would at any point in my life. He was the reason that people came to that place of business. He developed individualized, unique relationships with each customer in a fun and playful way. I would watch and see that everyone left with a better outlook than they came in with after they encountered Benny on each visit.

He mentored me in all aspects of the services provided. He taught me about quality and exceptional customer service. He would always do more than the customer had paid for. This has become a foundational part of my DNA in operating as a servant leader today. I was learning service that later became servant leadership."

Mark feels true servant leadership is a spiritual experience of connecting with people at a level of serving rather than leading.

"When I understood that my team members were actually my first line of customer, the servant leadership concept was taken to another level. Now we teach that we are each other's customer and put more emphasis on internal customer service."

Mark believes that a servant leader recognizes and celebrates the strengths of others and isn't tempted to force employees to do things their way. He uses a pertinent analogy to bring this point home.

"Be sure you do not cover your framework with someone else's framework when looking for the leader in you. Do not build your leadership on someone else's foundation."

CHAPTER 15: FROM TASKMASTER TO SERVANT LEADER

The story of David and Goliath illustrates Mark's point. When young David was poised to fight the giant Philistine named Goliath, King Saul tried to put his armor on David, but the armor was too big and clunky for him to wear. It would have stifled him and prevented him from victory. David chose to do what he knew best: take five stones and go into battle with a slingshot. Saul's armor was made to fit him, not David.

"Be careful that you are not trying to make your employees be like you. Each person has their own personality and working style. To enforce the exploitation of 'show up and I will tell you what to do,' some organizations add more management and control layers instead of empowering their workers. The more you disempower your staff, the more stress and pressure you put on yourself. Coach winners rather than just coaching people to win."

Mark describes it this way:

"Leadership is not at the expense of other people. Rather, it uses what is inside you to empower the next person. Empowering another person is like taking a piece of energy and transferring it to the next person. Each flame flickers entirely differently, although they are all lit from the same flame source. When you pass the energy of empowerment to the next person, do not expect it to look like yours."

COACHING AS SERVING ALL TEAM MEMBERS

Mark explains it like this:

"Sometimes I ask my Industrial Athletes who they are working for? I use this as a teachable moment.

They say, 'I am working for you.'

I try to help them understand that if I am serving and empowering them to achieve their desired earning rate, then that allows them to serve and perform for the customers for whom we manufacture, not just for me. It is actually an upside-down approach."

Mark continues:

"The Industrial Athlete plays various roles. First, they act as an industrial engineer, constantly evaluating the job and tweaking it to make it better and run faster. Second, they act as industrial entrepreneurs because they set their own performance-based rate. The coach comes underneath, lifts them higher, and helps them reach their goals and realize their full potential."

The role of the servant leader is illustrated in Figure 36.

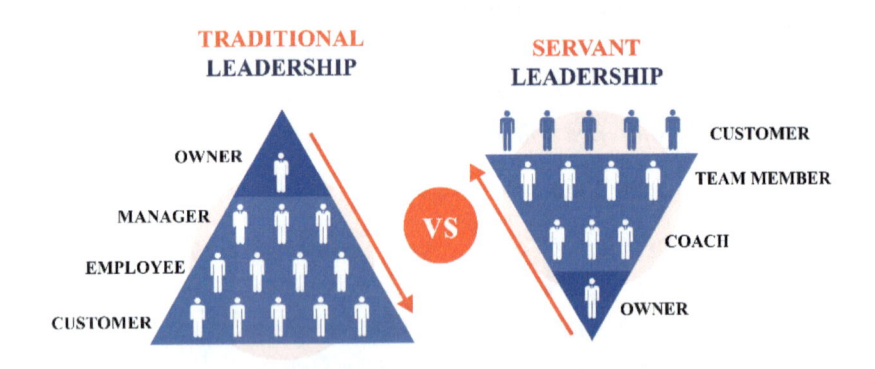

Figure 36: Servant Leadership Framework

The Industrial Athlete trusts that the coach can help them improve their skills and abilities and that they will be rewarded.

Industrial Athletes can achieve their highest accomplishment when they are in the state of mind that we call the *performance zone*. With this effective communication, the coach and the team members become aware of when they are in this zone. Communication is also necessary to deal with situations when people slip into a problem zone (a state of fight, flight, or freeze) that prevents effective communication and performance.

Living servant leadership the way he did, Mark laid the foundation for his son Brandon to follow in his footsteps.

CHAPTER 15: FROM TASKMASTER TO SERVANT LEADER

BRANDON AND AN EXAMPLE OF SERVANT LEADERSHIP

Brandon Lamoncha embodies the servant leader attitude needed to create an ecosystem rather than an egosystem. Brandon has experienced how other salespeople frequently look to wine and dine a prospective customer with an ulterior motive–a sales transaction. However, Brandon leads through relational service.

He was with a customer who happened to be a foundry manager. The customer could not focus on their meeting because his sand system was down. He told Brandon that he needed a specific part to get the system going again, so Brandon stopped the meeting and offered to drive him to the hardware store to get the part. The client was puzzled and wondered why Brandon would take the time out of his schedule to help him. Brandon said he understood that the customer wouldn't be unable to focus on the meeting while thinking about his production line being down–so they should go to the store, buy the part, install it, get the line running, and then talk.

Brandon has revamped Humtown's sales approach. The salespeople are more than just salespeople; they build relationships and find solutions for their clients.

A servant leader first tries to figure out what the customer needs, what troubles them, and what's going on in their lives. A salesperson sells products, while a servant leader provides solutions. Servant leaders learn how to figure out what is going on inside of the internal or external customer and match solutions to their needs.

As Brandon says,

"If you are there to meet people where they are, and they see that you are genuine and there to help, that is a ministry into the marketplace."

GREENLEAF AND THE SERVANT LEADER FRAMEWORK

The expression "servant leadership" was devised by Robert K. Greenleaf.[31] "The leader-first and the servant-first are two extreme types. The servant leader is servant first," Greenleaf says.

"It begins with the natural feeling that one wants to serve, to serve first. Then conscious choice brings one to aspire to lead. That person is sharply different from one who is leader first, perhaps because of the need to assuage an unusual power drive, or to acquire material possessions."

He explains more thoroughly,

"The difference manifests itself in the care taken by the servant-first to make sure that other people's highest priority needs are being served. The best test, and difficult to administer, is: Do those served grow as persons? Do they, while being served, become healthier, wiser, freer, more autonomous, more likely themselves to become servants?"

A servant leader demonstrates servanthood in their own life by surrendering their will. As a servant leader, I serve your best interest by lifting you.

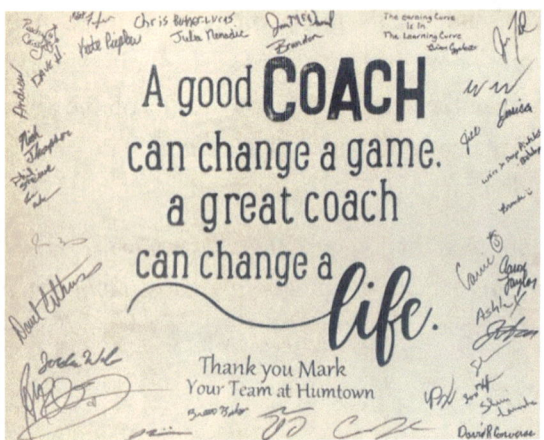

Figure 37: Humtown Team Members' Thank You

CHAPTER 15: FROM TASKMASTER TO SERVANT LEADER

Your Playbook: How You Can Make the Transformation

The role of servant leaders is a revolutionary one; they entirely flip the script on the conventional model of power leadership. The leader, who is responsible for serving the employees above them, is placed at the bottom of this new hierarchy. Servant leaders prefer it that way.

To be an effective leader of others, a coach needs to have credible influence, which comes from continually serving their team members and ensuring that they are aware that someone actually cares for them.

To assist with the transformation of taskmaster to servant leader, consider these points.

1. Have you become a servant leader who leads by example, modeling, and persuasion rather than by coercion?
2. Servant-leadership is at its core a value system; a value system that emphasizes the free-will and autonomy of each person.
3. Support coaches to foster individualized consideration for commitment.
4. Are the team members performing to the peak of their abilities?
5. Are coaches communicating assertively rather than passively or aggressively?

Notes

_____
_____
_____
_____
_____

CHAPTER 16:
FROM MICROMANAGER TO MULTIPLIER

"A person really doesn't become whole until they become a part of something bigger than themselves."

–Jim Valvano

The reason servant-leadership and inspire-and-trust coaching styles work is the multiplier effect. While traditional leadership involves the accumulation and exercise of power by one at the "top of the pyramid," servant leadership is concerned with sharing power and putting the needs of others first.[32]

The servant leader helps people develop and perform on as high a level as possible. As a result, people are empowered to multiply their efforts and make a bigger impact beyond their sphere of influence. The servant leader brings out the team's brilliance to accomplish more than the individuals can in their separate entities.

In contrast, a taskmaster often diminishes the team's talents, productivity, and well-being through micromanagement, implying that the team is inefficient, and that intelligence is rare and finite.

THE MULTIPLICATION EFFECT

We previously referred to the President of YSU, Jim Tressel, and his impact on our transition from employee to Industrial Athlete and from boss to coach. As a coach, he was a multiplier. Tressel's multiplication effect has impacted his coaching tree to the point that hundreds of his former assistant coaches and players are impacting various teams, universities, businesses, and government positions today.

The following story illustrates one example of the multiplication effect of leadership. Campbell Works in Youngstown shut their doors on Sept.19, 1977–a day labeled "Black Monday." Five thousand people who were employed by the steel mill lost their jobs, affecting their livelihoods and their futures.

That was just the beginning of the shutdowns that marked the era of deindustrialization in America–the same situation that, as we mentioned earlier, led to schools not teaching manufacturing classes and young people not being trained in manufacturing.

Youngstown experienced nothing but losses. There were fewer jobs and people were moving away. The only thing that increased was the crime rate. People who were once making a living could not make ends meet anymore. The tough time extended into the 1980s and 1990s.

By the time Coach Tressel arrived in Youngstown, poverty was at its worst and Youngstown's population had decreased significantly..

Tim retells a story.

"When I was in Jim Tressel's class for 16 weeks in 2013, I would wake up the next day completely inspired by the stories and array of world-class speakers he would bring in. The class was on a Wednesday night, and every Thursday morning, I would spring out of bed with energy for the day.

One of the stories Jim Tressel told touched me more than any other. Coach Tressel started coaching the university's football team in 1986. Five years later, in 1991, they were the underdogs to face the heavily favored Marshall Thundering Herd in Georgia in the national championship. Much to everyone's surprise and delight, YSU won the championship on national television.

They flew home and landed at Youngstown-Warren Regional Airport on a cold December night near Christmas. This airport does not get many flights; it is not a big airport. But when the team landed, they found a crowd of about two thousand people waiting for them out on the runway in the bitterly freezing weather. Nothing like that had ever happened before. The team disembarked and headed to the bus that would drive them to the university. As they walked through the crowd, everyone was cheering. There was

CHAPTER 16: FROM MICROMANAGER TO MULTIPLIER

energy and excitement as everyone celebrated their first national championship win.

As coach Tressel was about to get on the bus, someone grabbed his coat and pulled at him. He turned around to see an elderly man with tears streaming down his cheeks. The older man held up his fist victoriously and said, 'Coach, this is the best day I've had since VE Day.'

Meanwhile, because the remainder of the team was behind him, Coach Tressel was propelled into the bus, causing the man to let go of his jacket. Coach sat in the front row of the bus as it drove down Belmont Avenue, which went directly from the airport to the university. People were lining the streets, cheering, and honking their car horns as the bus drove past. When the team arrived at the university, more people greeted them.

Despite all the celebrations, Coach Tressel's thoughts were with the elderly man.

He retold, 'I am not a history genius, but I know one thing: VE Day, which was in 1945, was a long time ago. While driving on that bus to the university, I realized that the people of this town had not felt hope like they did that night in a long time.'"

Coach Tressel realized that the people of this region had not known the feeling of coming together and being inspired and energized in almost 50 years. The last time that elderly gentleman felt that much euphoria and excitement was after another great victory, when the Allies defeated the Axis Powers and Nazi Germany.

At that moment, Coach Tressel understood that the impact he had on his players, and his players' impact on others, goes beyond the 100-yard playing field—it multiplied like a ripple effect into the community. They changed the hope of a city. It inspired people to re-engage, and reemerge, allowing people to come out and celebrate again, get to know each other, network, work together, and find a reason for being. The win brought encouragement that gave people a spark to act in other areas of development.

Coach Tressel applied that motivation to his role as President of Youngstown State University to significantly increase his impact on the community in a greater way.

One of the ways he has done this is through partnering with industry leaders such as Humtown to increase career development of students K through 12, and build a pipeline not only into the university but into the workforce. Since taking office as Youngstown State's president, they have expanded their workforce education division and collaborated with Humtown and others to advance additive manufacturing. This has opened the doors to allow Humtown to integrate with professors, students, other university projects, and into the elementary schools.

YSU President Jim Tressel said,

"We are thrilled to partner with Humtown, America Makes, and others to bring this cutting-edge manufacturing technology to the region. Mark loves to talk about what it takes to be a good team member in the region where we can get our students, our faculty, our manufacturers, our thinkers, to all get together and work together.

Like any good partnership, there are several groups that will benefit from this venture, not the least of which are our YSU students, who will gain hands-on experience working side-by-side with industry and academic experts at this facility."

The example of going beyond the 100-yard field has also directly impacted Humtown to multiply their efforts outside of their own four walls.

Mark adds,

"Ahead of technology comes three-dimensional thinking and leadership; that's the kind of thinking and leadership we are seeing with YSU. As a team, including the expertise of YSU faculty and students, we look forward to refining this new technology, making the metal casting industry even stronger."

CHAPTER 16: FROM MICROMANAGER TO MULTIPLIER

The integration of education and industry used a brand-new 3D printer between Youngstown State, Penn State, and Carnegie for metal pouring. Mark says,

"We were able to integrate with students, interns, and professors on those projects. It inspired us to integrate into education, so now you have a new industrial thread starting with K through 12 and running through higher education. This is demonstrating what it is like to break down silos and integrate with the community."

MARK'S MULTIPLICATION OF LEADERSHIP THROUGH HIS COACHES

In the same way Tressel is a multiplier, Mark is one too. He has turned Industrial Athletes into coaches so that they can multiply their efforts and increase their performance, the performance of others, and ultimately, Humtown's performance.

Brian, Carrie, and Zach (who we've learned about as Industrial Athletes) have all moved on to multiply their efforts as coaches. Brian is the production coach for our VES location. Carrie is the production coach for additive manufacturing, and Zach is the production coach of new markets.

How Brian learned to multiply his efforts through others

While working as an Industrial Athlete, Brian moved over to work the afternoon shift. During that period, he had the opportunity to work more closely with Mark.

Since childhood, Brian had an issue with authority, and yet he gravitated toward Mark's leadership rather than running from it. He respected Mark's servant leader approach and how he treated people. In turn, Mark appreciated how Brian would bring ideas to the table. Mark, like his friend Sam Shinko, was willing to try something different and listen and help–even if it was not a promising idea. Mark trusted in the principle of First Attempt in Learning (FAIL) and allowed his Industrial

Athletes to FAIL forward. Brian had never seen that in any other owner, a quality that helped him decide that he would not leave Humtown to return to his former company. There was a greater opportunity at Humtown to learn and earn than at any other place where he had worked.

When Brian was asked to take a coach position, all his past authority issues surfaced. Because of a challenging upbringing, he ran away from sports and any other structured situation that involved instruction, direction, or supervision. He did not like that he had to obey rules or authority figures. He wanted the freedom to do what he thought was right and not have to follow some regimen or be boxed in by regulations. His lifelong mistrust of strict authority situations kicked in and he was concerned that becoming a coach would negatively impact his relationship with team members.

However, Mark's coaching style exposed Brain to a different side of leadership. He realized that he could serve and assist his team rather than "boss" them.

As a multiplier coach, if Brian saw a job running at 120% but he knew the rate could be better, he would demonstrate tips and tricks for success by taking over the machine for a couple of hours. Rather than push and prod, he would demonstrate what needed to be done to get the rate to 250%. Because Brian modeled the way, the Industrial Athletes were inspired to do it themselves, especially when Brian challenged them to knock his name off the top of the Top 10 List.

Several things come about when a coach does what Brian did. First, he *showed* the Industrial Athletes that they could do better rather than just telling them. He modeled trust and showed them how to improve their skills—thus multiplying his skill. When people learn that they can improve their skills at work, it has an overlapping effect—they recognize that they can grow in other areas of their lives. What they receive is confidence and support from someone they want to emulate.

CHAPTER 16: FROM MICROMANAGER TO MULTIPLIER

Carrie as a compassionate coach

After consistently performing as one of the top machine operators and filling in for the line coach when he was on leave, Carrie was promoted to assistant line coach. She later became a line coach and was then promoted to coach.

Although some tagged her as "caring too much" when she gave money to a rookie to buy steel-toed shoes, Carrie says she would buy everyone a new pair if she needed to—she is motivated by compassion.

Carrie doesn't enjoy a culture that is strictly business with no kindness. She lets people swap shifts or start earlier if they need to finish early, as long as it doesn't impact negatively on production.

One of Carrie's favorite sayings is,

"A little kindness doesn't hurt anybody."

Carrie went from a disengaged, often-absent employee to a coach who created fully engaged team members by caring about and acknowledging their talents. Her team members' engagement scores average over 90 percent in the area of team member satisfaction.

Zach's transition to inspire and trust

Zach needed to learn the coaching model on the job. He says

"The transition from the traditional boss model to the Industrial Coach concept was not easy, primarily because the idea was new to most management, and they did not know how to coach."

When Zach was asked to be a coach, he saw it as an opportunity to improve Humtown using his values and experience, thus multiplying himself, to help others become better. Zach was incredibly talented at fixing machines when he joined Humtown and usually went the extra mile. Humtown's VES was a radical boost to Zach's commitment to growth, which aided his emergence as a high-performing Industrial Athlete. Upon taking on the coach role, Zach focused on making training more hands-on and step-by-step. The role also taught him to use different communication methods with different personality types.

Team members were encouraged to help one another in the learning process, knowing that it would come back to them when they were the ones who needed help. Zach taught them that outstanding performance is more about learning and growing your skillset than pursuing an unhealthy rivalry with your colleagues.

Zach confirms there is not a single person on the floor who will not step in to help somebody who is having a problem. Team members take personal responsibility and help work towards a solution.

Zach says,

"Team members are willing to step in and help one another because they know they will be working with that person every day. They want a good working relationship–they might be working on the other side of the table from them tomorrow. If one team member is unwilling to take a couple of minutes to help another, then there may be no one to return the favor should the need arise. We are now family. We take care of each other."

HUMTOWN'S RESULTS

Coaching has proven to be far more productive, engaging, and stimulating than the command-and-control structure. Therefore, Humtown emphasizes and trains its supervisors and managers on the Industrial Coach and Industrial Athlete models as the most viable way to perpetuate high team member performance.

Coaches who multiply their efforts get the most from the team by multiplying their team members' talents. Our collective productivity skyrocketed from $60,000 per team member to more than $400,000 in production sales, as illustrated in Figure 38.

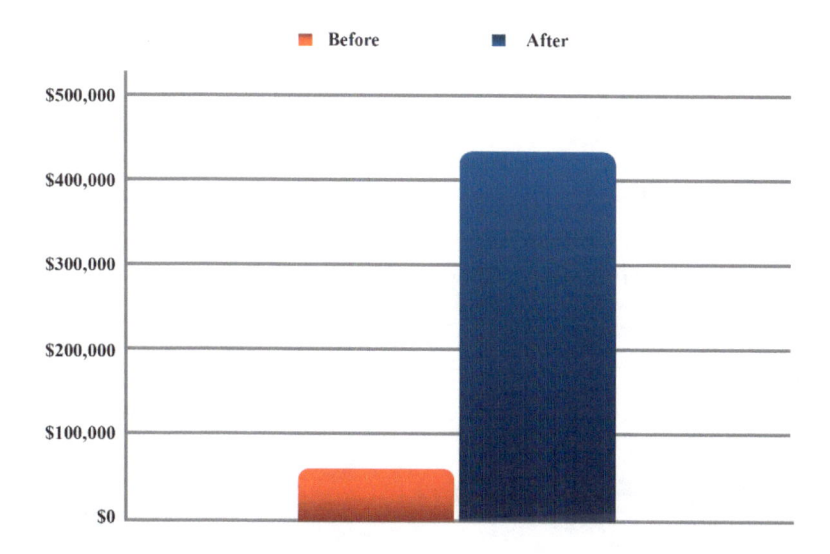

Figure 38: Monthly Sales Team Member Multiplication

Your Playbook: How You Can Make the Transformation

Multipliers are coaches who use their situation to amplify the talents, energy, and skills of the people around them; coaches who can cultivate their team members' intelligence by actively involving them. They are not concerned about receiving recognition, nor are they concerned with being the most outstanding person in the room.

Ask these questions.

1. How do your coaches develop and multiply the talents in your team members?

2. What are some strategies you can use?

3. Does everyone know what to do to achieve their growth goals?

Your Notes
_____
_____
_____
_____
_____

PART 4
CONCLUSION

Bosses control people rather than inspire them, leaving them unwilling or unable to think for themselves. Coaches encourage people to engage their heads, hands, and hearts. Coaches have many different jobs and do many different things. They must choose carefully which of these roles and activities will give them the best return. The main types of value that coaches can bring to their teams are additive and exponential.

When a coach adds their own knowledge and work to the group's efforts by doing a task or activity directly, they add value. So, their work is added to the work of everyone else on the team. Exponential value happens when the coach improves the skills or performance of other team members in some way, which makes the team stronger overall.

To turn employees into Industrial Athletes, a coach must align each person's skillset and successfully guide them to help the organization win. An Industrial Athlete does not need a boss; they need a coach to lift them up instead of suppressing their talents. As the Industrial Athlete's responsibility grows, so does their accountability.

The continuum below indicates boss-to-coach styles. Circle the one that most resembles you. Rather than being a tell-sell-yell boss who tries to control everything, be a coach that empowers decision making. Do you believe that the people who are closest to the decision are best equipped to make the decision?

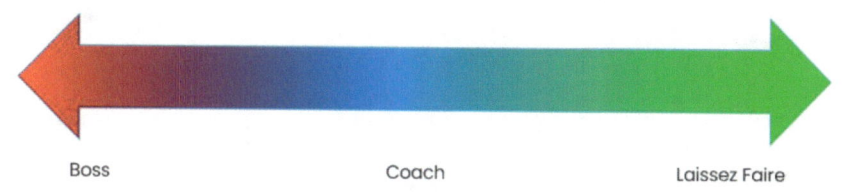

Figure 39: Coach Continuum

AFTERWORD: HOW TO TRANSFORM

With our roadmap, you can end the lack of engagement, end the high turnover, and create a workplace where your team has purpose, interest, passion, and engagement.

What would your workplace be like if you had a deeply engaged team? What could you achieve if you were all rowing toward a shared goal together?

Stop facing the exhausting tug-of-war between employees and managers. If you're ready to revolutionize your approach and transform how you lead so that you can unlock the value in your employees and create more value in your business, then implement the Industrial Athlete Operating System now.

Start with the assessment in Appendix A. In the same way there are individual and team sports, there are organizations that act more like an individual or team in the way they operate. This assessment is a benchmark for organizations to identify strengths and weaknesses and create a priority list for action steps.

THE INDUSTRIAL ATHLETE OPERATING SYSTEM FOR YOUR ORGANIZATION

If your organization wants a consultation, we first analyze its performance. Some organizations require a strategic plan, which is really about performance. Some organizations require an organizational culture assessment, and culture overhaul or remodel.

We can assess and transform the culture, or we can assess and develop your strategic plan and turn your workplace into a performance center.

We can assess and help the leaders work together, or to work to become better leaders. This includes management training or helping individuals make the personal transition by changing their mindset.

Do not be tempted to move forward in lockstep with anyone else who wants to implement the **Industrial Athlete Operating System**. Take the theories, strategies, ideas, and principles and meld them into something you understand and can apply to your business.

APPENDIX A: ASSESSMENT

THE WORKPLACE SHIFT:
FROM PLACE OF WORK TO PLACE OF PERFORMANCE

To facilitate a place where Industrial Athletes could thrive, we moved from the ambiguous expectations of the typical workplace to a place of performance. To do this, we focused on the differentiators of a performance-oriented environment: shared expectations, a relevant game plan, real-time feedback using technology with rewards, and ongoing training and practice.

From Chaos to Clarity: A Game Plan	☐ We are passionate about the mission of the organization, and have developed priorities to support our mission, vision, and strategy. ☐ We are clear about our specific set of core behavioral values. ☐ We have established Key Strategic (SMART) Goals as targets so that our priorities are converted into measurable action plans.
From Apathy to Engagement	☐ We report progress on activities and performance through a cadence of accountability. ☐ We take the time for ongoing training, cross-training, and skill building for team members.
From 4th-Quarter Failure to a Winning Scoreboard	☐ We have a scoreboard (KPI's, OKR's) that allows us to measure success and make sure we are on target to reach our goals. ☐ We have a Visual Earnings™ System (VES) to measure, motivate, and compensate team members for their performance.

THE CULTURE SHIFT:
FROM TUG-OF-WAR CULTURE TO A WIN-WIN CULTURE

Because culture impacts people and performance, we shifted from a tug-of-war hierarchy to building a high-trust ecosystem of win-win partnerships. To achieve this, we focused on four attributes of great cultures: inclusive stakeholder relationships, a climate of belonging and trust, a strong tradition, and a shared language.

From Us vs. Them to Win-Win	☐ We have a culture with win-win compensation that releases the collective capability of our team members and transcends their individual capabilities. ☐ We have a well-documented history, highlighting our individual and organizational accomplishments made visible to all stakeholders.
From Subtle Sabotage to Trusted Teamwork	☐ We have a way to measure whether our team members trust each other and the organizational climate. ☐ We survey all our identified stakeholders, to assure we receive their input and build trust.
From Downward to Upward Synergy	☐ We have identified a broad ecosystem that values all prospective stakeholders including Team Members, Economic Investors, Alliances, Marketplace Customers, and Society. ☐ We have recognition and reward systems that build the personal brands of team members and support the values and goals of the organization. ☐ We have a winner's manual that we use to create a shared vision, language, and standards that inspire persons for all aspects of their life (THRIVE 360).

THE EMPLOYEE SHIFT:
FROM EMPLOYEE TO INDUSTRIAL ATHLETE

To engage people to perform optimally, we need to shift from valuing employees in a one-dimensional view of productivity to valuing them like high-performing athletes. We focus on the same four areas that top athletes do: performing at their highest capacity, being fully engaged, developing their talent, and being a team player.

From Surviving to Thriving	☐ Team members have a sense of ownership by being fully involved, committed, enthusiastic, and active to thrive in performing in their tasks. ☐ Team members seem to have an overall sense of joy and fulfillment from being engaged in their everyday tasks.
Unique Talent	☐ We have a talent recruiting and onboarding pipeline that fits the person's interests and skills with the company's values and performance standards. ☐ Team members are made aware of and understand their unique interests, talent, and skills. ☐ Team members have the opportunity to creatively increase and develop their talent.
High-Performer	☐ Team members have the right amount of challenge that matches their skill level so that they are optimally performing. ☐ Team members receive feedback on what they are doing to help them stay on track.

THE MANAGERIAL SHIFT: FROM BOSS TO COACH

To empower team members to reach their best outcomes, we shifted from a supervisory management style, often leading to mistrust and disempowerment. We focused instead on the core elements of great coaching: mentoring, servant leadership, team building, and winning execution.

From Command-and-Control to Inspire and Trust	☐ Coaches intrinsically motivate and inspire their team members to help develop their talent and grow them into their full capacity. ☐ Coaches set a personal example of what they expect of others with a selfless attitude of service.
From Taskmaster to Servant Leader	☐ Coaches help team members clarify personal and team goals and action plans. ☐ Coaches manage change and gain agreement for buy-in to the organizational goals. ☐ Coaches help others through emotional or tense situations, tactfully bringing disagreements into the open and finding solutions all can endorse.
From Micro-Management to Multiplier	☐ Coaches encourage team alignment by finding the right fit for each person. ☐ Coaches support all team members to report activities and the measures of success through a cadence of accountability.

APPENDIX B: THE HUMTOWN STORY

1959: Humtown's family-owned legacy goes back three generations to Russell Lamoncha, who opened Humtown Pattern in Columbiana, OH. Russell and a partner operated the small pattern shop from a garage on the same property where the company is located today. Russell's son, Mark Lamoncha, grew up working in and learning the family business from a young age.

1977: When he took the helm, Mark wanted to expand the company, now named Humtown Products, beyond traditional pattern making. Mark was more interested in technology, innovation, and machinery. He was drawn to a new but related industry, sand core and mold production.

Still working

with foundries, they used a traditional blowing process to create air-set and cold-box sand cores and molds.

2008: Not long after the financial markets crash of 2008, Mark was desperate to prevent Humtown from going bankrupt. After much prayer, Mark created the framework of what would become the patented **Visual Earnings™ System**, a now-patented method of dramatically improving productivity by enhancing Humtown's workforce through technological innovation. This real-time process of measuring and showing team members' productivity rates would result in 250 to 400 percent sustained productivity increases.

2014: Humtown Additive is born, a division of Humtown that specializes in the additive manufacturing of sand cores and molds. Humtown received its first sand 3D printer in 2014 through a partnership with Youngstown State University. Since then, Humtown Additive has continued to add to its fleet.

APPENDIX B: THE HUMTOWN STORY   165

2018: As demand for Humtown Additive's 3D printed sand cores and molds started to explode, they quickly outgrew their manufacturing facility. In 2018, they moved out of their old facility into a massive 100,000-square-foot facility in Leetonia, OH. This gave them room to expand their 3D printer fleet and production capacity.

2020: A decade of relentless technological innovation at Humtown Additive culminated in 2020, when the company won the **National Association of Manufacturers (NAM) 2020 Manufacturer of the Year** in the small to medium enterprise category.[33] In making this selection, NAM's panel of expert judges cited Humtown's utilization and commercialization of 3D sand printing.

About Mark Lamoncha

Entrepreneur, Author, Inventor, Community Leader

Mark Lamoncha is an award-winning entrepreneur, inventor, author, and community leader. For more than four decades, he has been the president, CEO (Christ Empowered Owner), and head coach of the Humtown Products team.

He was featured on CNBC and continues to be visited by institutions such as MIT and the Fraunhofer Institute for his innovative, cutting-edge solutions. He and his company, Humtown Products, have become a national additive manufacturing pioneer by providing 3D sand printing while creating disruptive innovation to the foundry industry, resulting in partnerships with organizations such as the Small Business Development Center, Youngstown State University, Youngstown Business Incubator, and America Makes.

Mark invented the **Visual Earnings™ System** (VES) that helped his company win the **National Association of Manufacturers (NAM) 2020 Manufacturer of the Year** in four top categories alongside IBM, General Motors, and Peterbilt. He also has numerous patents.

He is a community leader focusing on education and charitable giving. He was appointed as a member of the Ohio Department of Education State School Board during the term of Governor Mike DeWine as well as to the Ohio Commodores. With a passion for career coaching, he spearheads integrating public education with business manufacturing.

Born and raised in Columbiana, Ohio, Mark and his wife, Sheri, have three sons (Brandon, Brenten, and Bronson) and are members of Greenford Christian Church.

About Dr. Tim Figley

Organizational Strategist, Author, Sports Broadcaster, Speaker

Dr. Tim Figley is an organizational strategist, sports broadcaster, researcher, author, and keynote speaker. He has facilitated strategic plans, family business transitions, and team retreats for hundreds of industry-leading nonprofits, family-owned and for-profit businesses. People have enjoyed his compassion, humor, and transformational insight for over a decade through his business and personal development presentations.

As a consultant, he has facilitated team development for the Human Resource team at the world's largest pallet supply company, and a culture-shaping initiative for the #1 community bank in Ohio. As an author, he has helped carefully craft the mix of business, leadership, and athletics into a practical, applicable business framework within the Industrial Athlete Program.

Dr. Figley is a researcher who received his MBA and Doctorate in Transformational Leadership from Bakke Graduate University. In addition, he has numerous certifications and accreditations in coaching and training by reputable worldwide organizations such as Marshall Goldsmith and Patrick Lencioni in Strategic Planning Facilitation, Mediation, Team Development, and Executive Coaching.

He has participated in charitable work for global missions in Africa, and he enjoys bike riding, whitewater rafting, cooking, and traveling with his two children, Zion and Miriam. His interest in sports has taken him to Super Bowls, The Masters, World Series, and All-Star Games with family and friends.

ACKNOWLEDGEMENTS

I want to begin by thanking my Heavenly Father and my relationship with Him through His son, Jesus Christ; for blessing me with my lovely wife Sheri, our spiritually inspirational relationship; and our three sons, Brandon, Brenten, and Bronson, who have all worked with me in this marketplace ministry at some point, while also moving on into other callings in their life.

To Sheri and the rest of my family for all of the time that people don't realize that it takes away from being a husband and father in order to be a responsible steward of a business.

To my parents, who have entrusted me with the responsibility of ministering to others in the field of manufacturing.

To all of my team members at Humtown that are family to me.

NOTES

[1] McKinsey Collection of Insights 2022, https://www.mckinsey.com/featured-insights/mckinsey-explainers/what-are-industry-4-0-the-fourth-industrial-revolution-and-4ir.

[2] Wikipedia, "Fourth Industrial Revolution," Wikipedia (Wikimedia Foundation, 2019), https://en.wikipedia.org/wiki/Fourth_Industrial_Revolution.

[3] SE Scholar, "Who Said 'the Whole Is Greater than the Sum of the Parts'?," 2019, https://se-scholar.com/se-blog/2017/6/23/who-said-the-whole-is-greater-than-the-sum-of-the-parts.

[4] Mitch Bannon, "The Most Watched Games in NFL History," Sportskeeda, 2021, https://www.sportskeeda.com/nfl/the-watched-games-nfl-history.

[5] Peter Thomson, "New Ways of Working in the Company of the Future," BBVA OpenMind, 2015, https://www.bbvaopenmind.com/en/articles/new-ways-of-working-in-the-company-of-the-future/.

[6] Patrick M. Lencioni, *The Five Dysfunctions of a Team: A Leadership Fable* (San Francisco: John Wiley & Sons, 2002), vii.

[7] Thomas Pyzdek and Paul Keller, *The Handbook for Quality Management: A Complete Guide to Operational Excellence.*, 2nd ed. (McGraw Hill, 2012), 35.

[8] Arbinger Institute, *The Outward Mindset: Seeing beyond Ourselves: How to Change Lives & Transform Organizations* (Oakland, Ca: Bk/Berrett-Koehler Publishers, 2016), 16.

[9] Craig Cherry, "Good Profit vs Bad Profit," The Loyalty Zone, 2020, https://www.theloyaltyzone.com/good-profit-vs-bad-profit/.

[10] KOSMOS, "Change Perception: Personal, Professional and Public," *Kosmos Journal for Global Transformation*, 2020, https://www.kosmosjournal.org/reader-essay/change-perception-personal-professional-and-public/.

[11] AZ Quotes, "John Wooden Quote," A-Z Quotes, accessed June 14, 2022, https://www.azquotes.com/quote/911837.

[12] Greater Cleveland Sports Hall of Fame, Inc., "Ginn, Sr, Ted," 2013, https://www.clevelandsportshall.com/ginn-sr-ted/.

[13] Ibid.

[14] Profiles Internationals, "Case Study: Setting Free Human Potential at Humtown Products," n.d., https://theprofilesgroup.com/case_study/Humtown_Products_Case_Study.pdf.

[15] Ibid.

[16] Thomas A. Holmoe, "Brotherly Love," BYU Speeches, 2006, https://speeches.byu.edu/talks/thomas-a-holmoe/brotherly-love/.

[17] Spirit Studios, "The Parable of Long Handled Spoons," Spirit Science Central, 2020, https://www.spiritsciencecentral.com/blog/the-parable-of-long-handled-spoons.

[18] Brad Spangler, "Win-Win / Win-Lose / Lose-Lose Situations," Beyond Intractability, 2013,

https://www.beyondintractability.org/essay/win-lose.

[19] Liyo Yu, "The Role of Trust in Team Building," Brighter Strategies, 2020, https://www.brighterstrategies.com/blog/the-role-of-trust-in-team-building/.

[20] Brayn M. Nozaleda, "Awareness, Acceptance, and Understanding of Cagayan State University Stakeholders towards Its Vision, Mission, Goals, and Objectives," *International Journal of Advanced Research in Management and Social Sciences* 8, no. 6 (2019): 313–26.

[21] Emily Kaplan, "Living the NFL Dream at Kurt Warner's Hy-Vee," Sports Illustrated, 2016, https://www.si.com/nfl/2016/01/31/nfl-super-bowl-kurt-warner-hy-vee-grocery-story.

[22] Ibid.

[23] "Kurt Warner," Wikipedia, 2022, https://en.wikipedia.org/wiki/Kurt_Warner.

[24] AZ Quotes, "John Wooden Quote," A-Z Quotes, accessed June 14, 2022, https://www.azquotes.com/quote/911837.

[25] Elaine Pulakos, "Selection Assessment Methods a Guide to Implementing Formal Assessments to Build a High-Quality Workforce," 2005, https://www.shrm.org/hr-today/trends-and-forecasting/special-reports-and-expert-views/documents/selection-assessment-methods.pdf.

[26] Gallup, *First, Break All the Rules: What the World's Greatest Managers Do Differently* (New York: Gallup Press, 2016), 99.

[27] Tanya Tandon, "A Study on Relationship between Self Efficacy and Flow at Work among Young Adults," *International Journal of Indian Psychology* 4, no. 4 (2017), https://doi.org/10.25215/0404.069.

[28] Charlotte Nickerson, "The Yerkes-Dodson Law and Performance," Simply Psychology, 2021, https://www.simplypsychology.org/what-is-the-yerkes-dodson-law.html#:~:text=The%20Yerkes%2DDodson%20law%20describes.

[29] Beth Cabrera, "Deep Work for Well-Being," Cabrera Insights, 2019, http://cabrerainsights.com/?p=4173.

[30] Profiles Internationals, "Case Study: Setting Free Human Potential at Humtown Products," n.d., https://theprofilesgroup.com/case_study/Humtown_Products_Case_Study.pdf.

[31] Robert K. Greenleaf, *The Servant as Leader* (The Greenleaf Center for Servant Leadership, Cop., 1970).

[32] Greenleaf Center for Servant Leadership, "What Is Servant Leadership?" 2021, https://www.greenleaf.org/what-is-servant-leadership/.

[33] Humtown, "Awards," accessed June 14, 2022, https://www.humtown.com/awards.

CONTACT US

For speaking engagements, book interviews, and workshops, please reach out to:

Mark Lamoncha
Email: mark.lamoncha@humtown.com

Tim Figley
Email: tim@timothyfigley.com

Additional Contact Information:
Phone: 330.482.5555

Mailing Address:
Humtown Products
44708 Columbiana-Waterford Rd.
P.O. Box 367
Columbiana, OH 44408

Made in the USA
Columbia, SC
25 June 2024